P9-BTN-768

Saving God's Green Earth

rediscovering the
church's responsibility to
environmental stewardship

Saving God's Green Earth

rediscovering the
church's responsibility to
environmental stewardship

TRI ROBINSON
with JASON CHATRAW

ampelōn
PUBLISHING

ISBN: 0-9748825-8-5
Printed in the United States of America
Third printing

Requests for information should be addressed to:
Ampelon Publishing
6920 Jimmy Carter Blvd., Ste. 200
Norcross, GA 30071

To order other Ampelon Publishing products, visit us on the
web at: www.ampelonpublishing.com

Cover & inside design: Lisa Dyches — cartwheelstudios.com

777

119621

DEDICATION

Authoring a book that attempts to communicate the responsibility for Christians to embrace the biblical mandate to care for creation has stirred a passion deep within me. It has challenged me to be courageous; it has generated faith to believe for what has seemed impossible.

As I look back over my life I am deeply grateful for the many people who have influenced me by exposing me to the grandeur and miracle of nature. I am grateful for a mother and father who took me backpacking and camping as a young boy; for a dad who took me hunting and fishing; for my life-long friend Pat Armstrong who taught me to pack a mule and see the poetry of the wilderness; for my wife who is always willing to take adventures; and for my two kids who challenged me to rethink my Christian responsibility in this area. I am thankful for my taskforce who worked so diligently to develop our church's environmental ministry; and for Jason Chatraw who enabled this passion to be put into written words.

Honestly, to dedicate a book that somehow expresses what's in our heart at Vineyard Boise concerning the miracle of creation – we would have to conclude that this book can only be dedicated to the author of creation himself – the author of our faith. In the final analysis, our dedication is simply to Jesus.

CONTENTS

INTRODUCTION

As I took the pulpit that morning, there were two conflicting emotions stirring within me—fear and excitement. I have preached many messages on controversial topics, but never one that could be so potentially polarizing to the congregation or detrimental to my position in ministry. However, I was also so excited about the opportunity and the momentum of the moment; I couldn't wait to see what was going to happen. Hopefully what I had seen in Scripture, heard from God, and read from well-respected Christian leaders from centuries ago was still relevant today. I couldn't be missing it, could I?

This message had the potential to be quite politically charged. It had everything to do with politics and nothing to do with politics. More than anything, it was about doing the right thing at the right time for both my church and my community. I had to shed my inhibitions and insecurities in order to be obedient to what I felt like the Lord was leading me to share with my church. How would the congregation respond? There was only one way to find out.

As soon as I finished my message, I was in for the shock of a lifetime. With my "great" faith, I thought the response could be anywhere from throwing me out on my ear to a tepid reception before a warm embrace. Never could I have imagined what happened next.

Instead of any of my worst or (admittedly limited) greatest expectations coming true, I watched in awe at the end of both services that morning as the congregation rose to their feet and applauded. Over my 25 years in ministry, that has never happened to me. I have received plenty of pats on the back or firm handshakes with an additional "atta boy" but never a standing ovation. It was in that moment that I knew this was more than a timely message. This was something that our church community on that particular Sunday morning had rediscovered as a responsibility. It wasn't something that was in conflict with their faith or even their political beliefs. It was shedding light on a responsibility the church not only has, but a responsibility the church has to be leading the nations in.

This was not just a random message thrown together on a whim. This was six months of cultivation and a lifetime in germination. When I initially realized the need to address this issue, I began to pray about how to tackle it and shared my thoughts with some of our leaders and staff. Together we began to devise a strategy on how to make sure that this wasn't just an inspirational message, because truly, it was a call to action. In no way did I want to stir the waters without giving people an opportunity to get wet. There had been far too much talk without action in this area within the church.

A month ahead of my anticipated schedule, I felt the timing was right. Our staff rushed around at the last moment to make sure all our opportunities were in place for our church. When I finished my message, I knew the applause meant nothing if they didn't vote with their feet. But vote they did. We saw a phenomenal surge that Sunday in the number of people who bought into what I shared, a surge that has turned into a snowball rolling down a hill with each passing week. No longer was this just a good idea to the people in our church—it was the right thing to do. It was their responsibility.

So, what was this message topic that could potentially create such a firestorm but instead united a congregation with passion? It was a Christian's responsibility to environmental stewardship. Simply put, the church must be diligent to tend the garden God has given us.

As you read this book, I hope it not only opens your eyes to the responsibility we have to be good stewards of the earth but also to the practical ways in which you can get involved in environmental stewardship within your own church and community. Plenty of churches have talked about the importance of the environment, but few have rolled up their sleeves and gone to work in the way that's necessary for conservation and renewal to occur. My prayer is that you will see this as a new way for Christians to live—and you will see how a new attitude in this area can save God's green earth in which we live … in more ways than one.

CHAPTER ONE

Rediscovering Environmental Stewardship

*The power of God is present at all places, even in the
tiniest leaf ... God is currently and personally present
in the wilderness, in the garden, and in the field.*

MARTIN LUTHER

*When I look at the night sky and see the work of
your fingers – the moon and the stars you have set
in place – what are mortals that you should think of us, mere
humans that you should care for us?*

PSALM 8:3-4

]was an Ecology major at the end of the 1960s during the height of the environmental movement, but eventually began a career as a school teacher. My wife Nancy and I spent the first 14 years of our marriage without electricity because we lived in an older home on our family ranch in southern California. We truly lived off the land; we grew some of our own food and always valued the natural balance of our surroundings. Because of that lifestyle, our two kids grew to know the worth of nature. But later in life when I became a Christian and entered into the ministry, somehow I disconnected from all of these values and affections. I never stopped loving nature, but it was somehow set aside because there was no real value for environmental stewardship in the church. The evangelical church in the 1970s was rife with a theology known as Dispensationalism, which implied—if not explicitly stated at times—that "Jesus is returning and the earth is going to burn up anyway, so go ahead and use it up." During that time, a lot of Christians—people who had once seen the value in cherishing and protecting the environment—lost their ideals and didn't see them as a value in the church, myself included.

Since 1989, I have pastored and led a church in Boise, Idaho, a place where God's beautiful creation surrounds you on every side. Outdoor recreation is a high value here. People hike, ski downhill and cross-country, mountain bike, fish, and hunt. But for years, I was always afraid to use the word "environment" because I didn't want to be labeled a "liberal." In the political landscape of the United States, environmentalism has always connected with a liberal perspective on the world. If you were a liberal, you were also supposedly for many other things that I simply could not accept or attach myself to. And while I shared many of the ideals of "conservatives," I viewed the environment as one issue that I could let slide. But that began to change when I realized I couldn't let political affiliation dissuade my higher allegiance to God's Kingdom, and from my charge as a Christian to be a good steward of all God's creation.

In recent election years, this issue struck close to home when we had political discussions with our grown children. As a result of the way they were raised by us, they have a strong love for nature. While I found choosing a political candidate to vote for relatively simple, they were conflicted. On one hand, they sided with candidates who stood for human rights and the right for all people to live, including the unborn. But on the other hand, they also strongly agreed with those who were dedicated to protecting the environment from destruction for the purpose of economic gain. And while most Christians in the United States today make the value judgment that human life is more important than plant and animal life (and rightly so), God still values both people and nature. This tension was keenly felt by both of our children and raised the question: "Why do we have to choose? Why can't the Body of Christ be for both?" After all, God is for both.

Both predominant political parties in the United States stand at odds over this issue, yet it simply remains an issue. Liberals are unable to gather the necessary support in the court of public opinion and through social action to actually make a difference. Conservatives and the evangelical church have, for the most part, avoided supporting the issue altogether. In taking a strong leadership role on this issue, the church must grow thick skin and help provide a solution rather than be frozen in fear over people's perceptions from either side of the political aisle.

A few years ago during a wedding reception at our church, I was cornered by a woman who asked me, "Are you the pastor of this church?" The tone with which she asked the question made me think maybe I didn't want to be at that moment! However, I confessed that I was and braced for whatever criticism she was going to hurl in my direction. "This wedding reception should be a crime," she stated matter-of-factly. "I've never seen so many items going to waste instead of going into recycling bins." I was embarrassed and tweaked by the stinging truth: I had not led our church in this area, thus we had no church-wide recycling program.

God had already been at work in my heart about the issue of environmental stewardship, but this incident began to push me toward taking action. While the pressing question was, "How can I make caring for the environment a value in my church?", the more troubling question for me personally was, "How did this once strong value in my life all but disappear?"

WHY GOD VALUES CREATION

All of God's creation is important to Him, down to the last sparrow and blade of grass. The story of mankind in the Bible begins in a garden and ends in a restored garden. The first commission to God's people is found in the opening chapters of Genesis, which exhorts us to be caretakers of the gift of creation. But why?

The first chapter of the book of Romans tells us that all of humanity knows there is a God because God has revealed Himself, and His very nature, through creation. God directed this assurance, this undeniable proof, to people who are struggling with the most basic spiritual issue: The very existence of a loving Creator.

As the Bible opens, the author of Genesis chronicles God's magnificent creations—man, woman, plants, trees, animals, sun, moon, stars, land, sky. With the creation of Adam, the scene shifts to the new garden, where the fall of humanity eventually occurs and introduces sin into the world. Suddenly, the garden was defiled. But as we read ahead—all the way to the end in the last book in Scripture, Revelation—we see the way God brings us back to a restored garden. The Bible begins in a garden and concludes in a restored garden. (See Genesis 2 & Revelation 22) Shouldn't this make us sit up and take note that there's something important about a garden, something that tells us God values the relationship between His people and the rest of His creation? If one of the ways God reveals Himself to people is through His creation, doesn't it stand to reason that we should share in His high value of caring for the environment?

Not only is creation an assurance, but its loving care is the biblical responsibility of God's people. One of God's first commands to mankind was to "tend His garden." And then, after the great flood, God made a covenant, not just with Noah, but between Himself, the earth and humanity. We refer to it as the Covenant of the Rainbow, an idea we'll explore more in-depth later.

DEFINING ENVIRONMENTAL STEWARDSHIP

As we seek to become good stewards of the environment, we have to define environmental stewardship. Environmental stewardship is the idea that we should care for, manage, and nurture what we have been given. Unfortunately, many people have become disillusioned by the way some environmentalists express their support for the earth, resulting in disdain toward any group or movement that cares for the earth. However, behavior such as spiking trees, eco-terrorism, or burning down houses in unwanted developments is not true environmentalism. That is a destructive brand of activism that leads to nothing but confusion and division about the true purpose and intention of their cause. In our desire to take a biblical perspective on environmental stewardship, we find four major areas that require our attention.

Resource and provision. The first thing we must understand is that environmental stewardship views nature as a resource and provision. More extreme environmentalists tend to contradict this idea because they don't have a biblical worldview. God has given us His creation to use, not to abuse.

God has given us his creation as a way of providing for people. Plants and trees produce fruits, vegetables, and herbs which are all healthy sources of nourishment for people and animals. Properly managed land is what sustains these plants to grow. Then the fruit of the land sustains human existence. It's a way God shows care for us through what He has created. Our day-to-day choices—how we manage the land with our crops, how we treat animals, and how we take care of our natural resources such as water and air is important because they are part of God's great plan for resourcing and providing for his creation.

Accountability. Secondly, there must be a balance between the use and protection of the creation. God has given us the responsibility for life on all sides. One thing that stands out to me while reading through the Old Testament, especially when the children of Israel were in the wilderness, is that God called Moses to be a game warden of sorts and protect the balance of creation. (See Deuteronomy 22:6-7) God calls people to be responsible in terms of game loss and make sure harvesting animals is done in a responsible way. An animal that becomes endangered because of human abuse is unacceptable. We must be accountable for the way we handle the delicate balance of nature.

Blessing. A third element of environmental stewardship is that of blessing. Environmental stewardship must look at God's creation as a blessing—something sacred. Whenever we see the splendor of God's creation, we stand in awe, slack-jawed at the beauty in a sunset or the creativity in a mountain range or the pure serenity surrounding a pond hidden away in the woods. It's in these moments that we realize how sacred these places are. It's a sanctuary for God's creation—a place where plants, animals, and people should be able to live together in harmony. And we should treat creation with such regard, showing reverence toward the One who created it by making sure others have the opportunity to experience the unspoiled wonders as we have.

Passing it down. A fourth aspect of environmental stewardship is its intergenerational nature. Stewardship is a value to be passed from generation to generation, emphasizing the great importance of caring for God's creation. Most of the values we adopt from our parents are "caught," actions and behavior we observe and absorb. What our parents *say* to us is important, but what they *do* leaves an indelible mark on who we are as we grow up and mature.

At our church, heritage is an important element in our ministry philosophy. We want people to understand that following Jesus isn't something you simply do—it's part of who you are. And when it becomes part of who you are, it's something you naturally desire to pass down to the generation behind you. As our church began to weave heritage into the fabric of our faith, realizing that this value was of great importance to walking out what it means to be a follower of Jesus, we presented many opportunities for people to get involved. And one of the ways that enabled parents to pass stewardship values down to their kids was through organized camping trips, where many parents took their children into the woods with other families for wilderness cleanup and restoration projects. Kids were seeing first-hand ecological values being lived out by their parents. When we model how to steward what God has given us, our children will catch the lifestyle and it will become part of who they are.

PASSING IT DOWN IN BOISE

Before I first started teaching on the importance of environmental stewardship in my church, one of the things I did was gather a group of specialists into a "secret" task force. People in our community love the outdoors and care for it passionately. I knew men and women in our church who worked with the U.S. Forest Department and the Fish and Game Department as well as various other areas of outdoor recreation. While I hadn't really heard them express this to me, I knew they were people working in the area of conservation who identified themselves with the call and mission of Jesus.

As we began to explore what it means to be good stewards of the environment, two men from the Parks Department brought me a shocking statistic: They said in the past 10 years in the state of Idaho, there was one-third less exploration of the state's wilderness area. At the same time, there was a one-third increase in the state's population. This puzzled me. How could Idaho, which has the largest wilderness areas in the continental United States, experience such a decline with an inverse boom in the population? It didn't make sense. Then, the reality hit me that fathers have quit taking their children hunting, fishing and hiking. More kids were sitting in front of the television playing video games on the weekend. And the families who were getting out weren't doing so in the traditional sense—they were going in vehicles or machines where they couldn't possibly hear nature and were probably going too fast to appreciate it. I know that what people don't see, they can't appreciate. And what they don't appreciate they won't value. People weren't getting into the mountains.

One of our strategies was to get the people in our church outside the city limits where they could see the stars at night and the beauty of their surroundings. Many of them had not seen it because of their lifestyle. I realized in order for the environment to become a value in the church, it had to be experienced individually and passed on generationally.

While the components of environmental stewardship seem simple enough and make good sense as we shall soon see, why has the church in the Western world today refused to embrace these simple values?

MISLED BY FEAR

I believe many Christian leaders, myself included, have been fearful of what might happen if we actually advocate something that has been decisively tagged as a value that belongs to those who oppose many Christian values. In our fear, we have been unfaithful to our responsibility to be good stewards of God's creation. Because of my desire to stay bipartisan I stayed away from the issue altogether for many years, viewing environmental conservation as a political hot button. But apathy toward the environment doesn't mean we have avoided getting involved in the issue—it simply means we have decided its value is not worth fighting for. And this is where many evangelical Christians in the United States have gone awry.

In one sense, it's hard to blame Christians who experienced the environmental movement of the 1960s. We saw hypocrisy in the "earth first" approach and it seemed meaningless. The whole "mother earth" theology took no one to God—and this had the effect of polarizing us from our neighbors who expressed any kind of ecological concern, blinding us from theologically sound and practically balanced approaches. However, it's getting more and more difficult to ignore the signs that the earth is under siege by gross human mismanagement.

Over and over again, evil has a way of stealing things out of God's camp, values that the church is called to champion. As a result of the Western church's apathy toward the environment, much of the world perceives the church as championing a way of life that is destructive to the planet. And in the United States many people perceive the church as conservative and therefore intimately allied with the Republican Party, which is more interested in capitalistic strength than environmental stewardship when it comes to managing our beautiful country. One environmentalist remarked in obvious irony: "It's interesting that conservatives are the least likely to support conservation." I believe it's time Christians begin to rediscover the values we have lost and be on the leading edge of promoting environmental stewardship with practical instruction on how to implement these ideals in our daily lives.

One environmentalist remarked in obvious irony: "It's interesting that conservatives are the least likely to support conservation."

OUR FUTURE IN MIND

In implementing the value of environmental stewardship into our lives, we will make a necessary shift from thinking about the here and now to thinking about the future. As a member of the Baby Boomer generation, I have seen firsthand how people in my generation have made shifts from short-sighted thinking to serious reflection on the future with the addition of each generation to their own families. When people have their first child, this tends to initiate a sudden transformation in the way they view the world around them. New parents begin to ask some challenging questions: Will the world be safe for my kids? Will my children have all the same opportunities that I did? Will they be able to succeed? Will they have all the same freedoms I have? Will they be able to enjoy life the way I did?

As we have seen the earth abused and misused, those same questions are being asked about the environment, sometimes with much regret by the same people who unknowingly failed to think about the future of the earth. It's why Jesus did what He did; he came to earth to live and die for the sake of mankind—and indeed, the entire cosmos—for eternity. Failure to adopt this future-driven element in our thinking—and subsequently, our actions—may result in a missed opportunity to experience a revolution in our own hearts as well as in the world around us.

> Failure to adopt this future-driven element in our thinking—and subsequently, our actions—may result in a missed opportunity to experience a revolution in our own hearts as well as in the world around us.

One powerful example of a leader in the Bible who failed to think about the future was King Hezekiah. In 2 Kings 20, we find him confronted by the prophet Isaiah, who informs the king that some of his descendants are going to be exiled to Babylon. And Hezekiah's short-sighted reaction was this: "At least there will be peace and security during my lifetime" (vs. 19). He was more concerned about his current popularity than his eventual legacy.

The moment is right for the church to reverse its wrongs in the area of environmental stewardship. By abandoning our short-sighted thinking and returning long-term vision to the church, Christians have an opportunity to change things. It won't be easy. Many people from both liberal and conservative camps alike are likely to cast a suspicious eye on such a sudden reversal of position. But if the statistics are true and one-third of the world is comprised of Christians, what would happen if one-third of the world became serious about upholding the value of environmental stewardship? This would make a difference. This would change the world.

Dennis Mansfield: A Passion Reignited

In the 1980s, being a Christian and an environmentalist didn't seem like a conflict in values for Dennis Mansfield. He owned a hydro-seeding, hydro-mulching company that covered millions of square feet with its reforestation projects. Being located near a forest that was burned, Mansfield worked hard to restore the environment. "As a conservative, I found that being environmentally sound was actually good business," Mansfield said.

But that was before he went to work for a Christian ministry. Over the ensuing 15 years, Mansfield learned that it was best not to share his views on the environment lest he draw the ire of his fellow co-workers. "Whenever I would speak to those in the evangelical community about environmental issues, I always got this long and leery-eyed look from people and they would ask, 'Oh, are you one of them?'" Mansfield said. "I used to think, 'Well, what am I?' I am one of 'them' in terms of making sure that environmental stewardship ought to occur. But I learned to be very quiet for years and just did my job."

But something happened to Mansfield when he began hearing that his church might begin starting a ministry that focused on caring for the environment. "I had just let my passion for caring for the environment lie dormant for so long," Mansfield said. "But then I had it really re-awakened when some people of faith challenged me. That began to awaken my heart again for this passion that was all but lost.

"When my pastor brought out his heart's desire that we could bring people together with an environmental background and do something about it ... I realized it wasn't the next step in some plan to make the church look good in the community, but it was really at the heart of the church's values. Though everybody who was involved in the initial stages of this ministry had cared for the environment individually, we had never been given the opportunity to discover it corporately."

While Mansfield has been on both sides of the fence, he now wonders why there are two sides of the fence at all when it comes to caring for the environment in a responsible way. "It's always been perceived somehow, in some way that the church and those who care for the environment were at odds with each other," he said. "I'm an evangelical and thankful for my faith in Christ—and I care about the environment. But at the same time, I felt like I was on the fringe."

But Mansfield believes that the church has the opportunity to change people's thinking about the environment and take the kind of action necessary to result in lasting change. "I think the church really is the missing link between government agencies that are out there and those who receive full-time compensation to do it.," he said. "Government agencies do a good job, but it's surprising how much more help they need. Care for the environment, by in large, has been stirred through emotions. Many people say, 'I just feel good about caring for the environment.' Well, that's great, but this is where the church can challenge people to say, 'Well, why don't you come on out and pick up a shovel and help us?' It's that change in thinking about the environment that will challenge both liberals and conservatives, people of faith and people without faith."

And if the church were to really warm to this concept of environmental stewardship, Mansfield thinks the planet as we know it would change for the better. "If the entire church across North America were to embrace this, it would be a huge paradigm shift. · We believe that creation is vital and we've been given the stewardship right to be involved in it—and we're obviously starting to cultivate it in a direction that honors God.

"I think if Christ was here today as a carpenter, he would be caring where the wood came from. Let's care about the environment. We need to be those people who follow in Christ's steps. It's not a weirdo-religion thing; it's a wonderful relationship thing where churches across the U.S. can care for their own section of the environment and do it together."

While the topic may still be sensitive in many Christian circles and stir heated debate, Mansfield encourages believers to put aside preconceived ideas and think about what God is truly calling people to do. "To the Christian who is conflicted about the issue of the environment and is afraid to rock the boat but really does understand there's something in his heart that says, "I really want to go for this," I say, 'Rock the boat!' Be Peter. Get out of the boat. But do it humbly, in a way that says, 'I'm not going to let anyone dictate what I believe outside of the word of God.' He made this earth and it's good. It's really good."

CHAPTER TWO

Finding the Creator in His Creation

These creatures minister to our needs every day: without them we could not live; and through them the human race greatly offends the Creator. We fail every day to appreciate so great a blessing by not praising as we should the Creator and Dispenser of all these things.

FRANCIS OF ASSISI

From the time the world was created, people have seen the earth and sky and all that God made. They can clearly see His invisible qualities – His eternal power and divine nature. So they have no excuse whatsoever for not knowing God.

ROMANS 1:20

A s a 16 year old, I found myself sitting on the side of a mountain watching the sun set across the vast Mojave Desert one evening. My parents had just given me a 1956 Volkswagen Bug—more than likely because the motor was about as powerful as a sewing machine and accelerated speeds were impossible—and I had my freedom to go be all alone for one of the first times in my life. It is unusual for a teenager to seek out a place as remote as this was, but I had deliberately gone there to find the answer to some of life's deepest questions. I wanted to know if God existed, if creation was God's doing, and if my life had purpose in it at all.

I was raised in a Christian home and somewhat understood the reality of God in the Bible. I had read about the miracles in the Bible as well as Jesus' birth, life, ministry, death and resurrection that had been prophesied for thousands of years before His coming. I heard that Jesus had perfectly fulfilled every prophecy and how this had been witnessed firsthand by the apostles and recorded in the New Testament. But that night, I was asking for more.

As I sat on that mountain, I was asking the most important question of the ages. I wanted to know for myself if God really existed and if my life really mattered. Maybe it was because I was alone and sincerely asking real questions (Jesus did say, "If you seek, you will find"), but on that evening as I looked across the breath-taking landscape before me, I came to the amazing reality that it was all true; God must exist. I recognized God in His creation! In the inspiration of the moment, I found a small piece of paper and scratched a few words on it trying to communicate what I had discovered in my heart. Though I haven't kept many mementos from my youth, I still have that particular piece of paper. The words on it are a bit flowery, and I must confess that I'm somewhat embarrassed to share them—but here they are:

And the voices roared, "Too little proof!"
And I replied, "I have broken from the dense pines,
and there I have smelled the sap and grasped the earth.
I have heard the silence and lifted my head to it
and as far as I could see, there was beauty;
swift shadows of clouds on silver fields, the colored sunset,
the jagged Sierras smothered into the endless deserts."
And now I say, "Haven't I seen the face of the Lord?"

Years later, I read what the apostle Paul said about how God reveals Himself through nature, and because of it, we are without excuse from acknowledging God's existence. In the first chapter of the book of Romans, Paul wrote, "For since the creation of the world God's invisible qualities—His eternal power and divine nature—have been clearly seen, being understood from what has been made, so that men are without excuse." Paul told us that not only had God revealed Himself through Scripture and the witnessed ministry of Jesus, but God also revealed Himself through nature. The environment is a major assurance to mankind of God's existence and yet it is an assurance that has been overlooked and neglected in recent years by many Christians.

FINDING GOD IN NATURE

Hundreds of stories have been told and many tales have been spun about St. Patrick, the patron saint of Ireland, beginning with the fact that he was born in Britain, not Ireland. However, one of the most fascinating stories surrounding St. Patrick's mission to Ireland after being held there in captivity as a young man was how he shared truths from the Gospel with a culture that strongly identified with the environment.

While living in Ireland and spending so much time in nature, Patrick recognized the beauty of God's creation all around him; therefore, it was easy for him to use nature to communicate the heart of the Gospel with the people. Patrick realized it was the way to their hearts; it was the way to show them the assurance of God's existence. Instead of condemning the Irish people's love for nature, he incorporated many cultural rituals into his teachings. One Irish tradition was to honor gods with fire. So, Patrick used bonfires to celebrate Easter. To a nation steeped in this tradition, it simply made sense to honor God this way.

> Instead of condemning the Irish people's love for nature, St. Patrick incorporated many cultural rituals into his teachings.

One of the most recognizable symbols from Irish tradition is the Celtic cross, which was another way Patrick used their love for nature to show them Christ. By superimposing one of the Irish's most powerful symbols—the sun—onto the Christian cross, the new Celtic cross seemed to carry more weight. Patrick wasn't watering down the Christian faith; rather, he was contextualizing the Gospel for a group of people who could already see God's creation all around them—they just didn't know the Creator. In fact, the most well-known symbol regarding St. Patrick's Day is the clover, of which Patrick used its three leaves to point to the Trinity.

EARNING THIS VALUE BACK

However, St. Patrick had no political biases to work through. The beauty of nature was all around him—and the people of Ireland simply celebrated it. Oftentimes, it is difficult to differentiate between agendas and truth when it comes to hearing about Christian causes in which we should get involved. After all, there is no better way to spread a message than through the church. But in the church, we must be faithful gatekeepers to ensure that the messages entering into our churches are founded and wrapped in biblical truth, not merely riding on the coattails of Scripture.

The political overtones associated with caring for the environment are difficult to shake, but stewardship of the earth emerges from such a fundamental tenet of the Christian faith that we cannot ignore it.

The political overtones associated with caring for the environment are difficult to shake, but stewardship of the earth emerges from such a fundamental tenet of the Christian faith that we cannot ignore it. Instead of disposing of nature, St. Patrick was undoubtedly inspired by the Holy Spirit to share the Gospel through it. In fact many men and women throughout Christian history have recognized God's beauty in creation, not as something to be worshiped but as something to care for. Consider this statement:

> Let all regard themselves as the stewards of God in
> all things which they possess. Then they will neither
> conduct themselves dissolutely, nor corrupt by abuse
> those things which God requires to be preserved.

This statement was not made by someone stretching to link our responsibility to steward God's earth with the Bible. It was made by a man who had a tremendous impact on the Christian faith centuries ago: John Calvin. He understood we must accept the charge to care for what God has created. He also understood the deep connection between the Creator and His creation, for it was in God's creation that we see God.

In his book, *Pollution and the Death of Man: The Christian View of Ecology*, Dr. Francis A. Schaeffer had this to say about how Christians should view their relationship to nature:

> On a very different level, we are separated from that
> which is the 'lower' form of creation, yet we are
> united to it. One must not choose; one must say
> both. I am separated from it because I am made in
> the image of God: my integration point is upward,
> not downward; it is not turned back upon creation.
> Yet at the same time I am united to it by the fact that
> both nature and man are created by God. This is a
> concept that no other philosophy has. ... This rela-
> tionship should not only be for aesthetic reasons—
> though that would be enough reason in itself—but
> we should treat each thing with integrity because
> this is the way God has made it. So the Christian
> treats 'things' with integrity because we do not
> believe they are autonomous.

More than 30 years ago, Schaeffer penned those words as he was troubled about the direction and attitude people took toward the environment. Even more troubling to him was the view that Christians were taking on the issue. He even went as far to say that Christians have missed a great opportunity to show the world how to care for the earth in a balanced way as well as reaching many people with the Gospel.

While the opportunity to both lead in the proper care for the environment and to share our faith in the process may have been suppressed because the issue was strongly linked to a "liberal" outlook on life, it's never too late to begin taking up this charge to steward the earth. However, the church cannot simply take back this issue; it has to earn it back. In leading the way, the church must win back trust from others who have seen the apathetic view of the church toward the environment result in the destruction of nature.

> The church cannot simply take back this issue; it has to earn it back.

For years, artists and poets have found ways to express the beauty they find in God's creation. It is one thing every person on the planet can appreciate. So, it is no wonder why people look at the church with disdain when the topic of the environment arises. Why wouldn't the church be leading the charge in keeping a portrait of God's beauty as close to pristine as possible? Why wouldn't the church preserve it in its purest form? For it's in nature that we oftentimes see not only the beauty but also experience the real presence of God.

THE ASSURANCE OF JESUS

Ten years after I had that experience on the mountainside and began seeing God's creation and recognizing there was a Creator, I found myself there again, confronted with a question whose answer would go a long way in determining the path my life would take. While I had come to the realization that there was a Creator, I still struggled to accept that Jesus was the Son of God and that God was the Creator.

At that time, Nancy and I were living on our family's ranch in California, raising our kids and enjoying life. Nancy came into a relationship with Christ a few years before and was fervently praying for me—an oblivious young dad in my late 20s—to come into a full understanding of who Jesus really was.

Before I found my way to the mountainside that evening, Nancy took me to a musical at a church about an hour away from our ranch. During the musical, there was a multi-media presentation that made a lasting impact on me. Now, you must realize that this was in the mid 1970s, and the cutting edge of media in those days were two slide projects that faded in and out simultaneously. During the presentation, the choir performed a song taken from Psalm 42 where David was crying out to the Lord, "As the deer pants for water, so my soul longs for you." As they were signing this song, the slide projectors would fade in and out images of nature. However, the projector kept returning often to this one picture of a doe with this deep penetrating gaze. For me, the deer represented Jesus—and that image grabbed me like no other. I was so taken by that picture, realizing that the longing in my heart was to come to know God and know for sure that Jesus was

God. I wanted to know it was really true.

Upon returning to our ranch that evening, I was so bothered by that picture that I was unable to sleep. I just wanted to spend some time and think. So, I returned to the same knoll on the mountain where I had sat when I was 16. As I approached the knoll, I noticed there was a log there in a clearing. After I sat on the log, I began praying, "God, if you're real and Jesus is your son, would you reveal yourself to me?" At that point in my life, I did not question the assurance of God, but I was still wondering about Jesus.

As I was sitting on the log praying, I heard footsteps behind me. I was terrified. I had lived in the mountains most of my life and it wasn't unusual for me to take walks in the night and hear strange noises. But on this particular night, I was terrified. Never mind the lions and tigers and bears. I was asking God to come and reveal Himself to me—and in my heart and my mind, I felt like God was walking up behind me, so much so that I was afraid to turn around.

With this paralyzing fear keeping me firmly seated on the log, I hardly moved when a deer stepped within an arm's reach over the log I was sitting on. She walked over the log, moved around in front of me and turned, looking me square in the eyes, just the same way the deer had stared at me throughout that multi-media presentation. It was in that moment that Jesus was really revealed to me. It was as if He was saying, "I'm here and I'm real—and I'm answering your prayer." I no longer needed any more assurance that Jesus was God's Son. I knew it deep in my soul.

THE ASSURANCE OF THE HOLY SPIRIT IN NATURE

In studying the Bible, we discover that finding God through nature is actually quite common. He came over some people like a mighty rushing wind. Others expressed their time with God like a refreshing river. Still others cried out their desire to know the Lord like rain in a dry and dusty land or an oasis in the desert.

In the early 1980s after being assured that Jesus was real through my experience with the deer, I had become a Christian and was really zealous about my faith. I wanted all God had for me. While I was growing in my faith, I knew that I wasn't experiencing the fullness of God. One evening, I attended a Bible study at my church, and the pastor was sharing about the Holy Spirit. He explained how the Holy Spirit empowered believers for a life of ministry and purpose. Near the end of his teaching, he explained how we can be empowered by the Holy Spirit, offering an opportunity for people to pray and ask the Holy Spirit to fill their lives. I had a hunger for God, and I believed that if God had more, I wanted everything.

I went to the front of the church that night and some young excited Christians began to pray for me. I remember feeling nothing and began to be put off by the whole process. But I was still very taken with the idea I had seen in the Bible that the Holy Spirit wanted to empower believers in serving God.

As I returned to our ranch that night bothered again by the events of the evening, I walked up the mountain and sat on a fence and began to pray. As I was praying and looking up toward the mountain, I said, "God if your Holy Spirit is real and I can be empowered by Him, then I want Him. I want all you have for me." It was a still, calm night on a beautiful evening, but that was about to change. All at once at the top of the mountain, I heard a wind coming down through this canyon above me. I could hear it getting closer and closer. It sounded almost like a freight train rolling down the hill. The noise got louder and louder as the wind approached. Almost instinctively, I took an extra hard grip on the fence. For a moment, I didn't know what to think. I was halfway terrified because I had just prayed that the Holy Spirit would come upon me, and I had also just read in Acts that the Holy Spirit came like a mighty wind. I thought God was coming down the mountain—coming to get me! When that wind hit me, all the hair on the back of my neck stood straight on its end. Then, as quickly as it had come, it was gone and the night was calm again. I can't say there was anything that manifested in my life that night, but I will say that my life was transformed from that day forward, marking the beginning of my zeal for ministry.

> God speaks to all of us in many different ways, yet it's through nature that He so easily grabs our attention.

God speaks to all of us in many different ways, yet it's through nature that He so easily grabs our attention. Among other things, Jesus primarily saw nature as a way of illuminating the Gospel and elements that are central to our faith. Parables of seeds, crops, soil, and trees abound in Jesus' teaching, unfolding deep spiritual truths and revealing elements about God's nature. In those days, people understood what it meant to work the soil to produce a crop. If there's so much beauty in nature and we experience God speaking to us through it, doesn't it make sense that the church should lead the way in caring for the environment? If we don't, we might just miss the greatest opportunity to share the Gospel that we've known in the 21st Century.

Dr. Calvin B. DeWitt:
Reading God's Two Great Books

Growing up in a home where both the Bible and creation were viewed as God's revelation, Cal DeWitt was surprised when attending a school friend's daily vacation Bible school. He realized that not all Christians viewed creation as something that needed to be cared for.

"During my upbringing my parents, teachers, and pastor impressed upon me the importance of the Bible as the Book of God's Word and creation as the Book of God's Works," he said. "So, I quite naturally came to see the study of creation as a worthy calling before God. In fact, in my church, school, and college I was encouraged to develop all of my gifts, including gifts in Bible study, theology, music, art, and science. It was wonderful growing up, since I was encouraged to behold creation and study the Scriptures coherently. Because of my interest in both the Bible and in creation, it was quite expected by my schoolmates, parents, pastors, and professors that I would eventually do work in life that involved study of creation, perhaps I would even become a scientist.

"Since God is the author of the Bible and of the whole universe, the study of both together is clearly a wonderful privilege and a marvelous way to bring praise to my Creator and Savior. Study of the creation became for me a calling—literally, a vocation."

In his late teens and early twenties, Cal viewed with bewilderment good Christian folks he came to meet who were skeptical about the worth of studying creation, and even more so people who seemed to care very little for the creation, other than it being a "bag of resources" to be tapped for consumption. It was this bewilderment that

45

helped stimulate him to become an effective and passionate teacher—a person who would profess both the truth of God's Word and the creation's testimony to God's divinity and eternal power. After all, he had embraced both faith in God and the wonders of God's creation at a young age. "My love for creation and God as Creator began with a turtle I kept when I was three years old—and in time my family's modest home in the city featured a backyard zoo and basement menagerie that grew in size and species throughout my youth and college years," he said.

With the encouragement of his father and mother, DeWitt pursued his love for ecology. This brought him from thinking that he might be able to run a pet store, to becoming a zoo director and then, earning him a Ph.D. in Zoology from the University of Michigan in 1963. As his love for animals involved increasing study and research, he found that he had become a professional—and professing—scientist. During a year off from graduate study between his masters and Ph.D., he taught Biology and Natural History at Calvin College, and in this discovered that he loved to profess his love for God and God's works as a teacher and professor. This eventually brought him to become a professor first at the University of Michigan and later at the University of Wisconsin.

It was during his doctoral research in the deserts of southern California that Cal began to realize that something was amiss with the way people were living in God's creation. "As I did pioneering research on discovering how the Desert Iguana survived and regulated its body temperature in an environment where in summer the surface temperature of the soil exceeded 170 degrees Fahrenheit, I saw disturbing things begin to happen in the desert around me as human construction laid waste to natural habitats," he said. "During the course of my research, I learned that my study site in the open desert was to become a new city—Palm Desert,

California. There was no water anywhere; my lizards managed to live without it; and the yearly rainfall of 2.54 inches was just enough to bring some sparse and faint greening to the desert for a week or two during the year. As I watched this 'development' unfold, I reasoned that this was not very wise—not very earth-wise," said Cal, concluding the project had not been conceived from a respectful reading of the creation's landscape whose text is so plainly written in the canyon, its alluvial fan, crisp dryness, and remarkable heat.

Intent on being "earth-wise" as a careful teacher and reader of the book of God's Works, Cal wrote a book for churches and church discussion groups entitled, *Earth-Wise: A Biblical Response to Environmental Issues*. Upon his return to the desert several years later he found his study site now covered by the approach pad to a drive-in bank, cattails growing in a drainage way along one of the streets downtown, water-misters spraying down from awnings of the downtown shops; and the desert iguana now found only in the Palm Desert Zoo.

"My science and the Christian faith were always interacting in an integrated and coherent way," he said. "That interaction grew substantially as I came to realize that we as human beings were proceeding to destroy the beautiful world that God created." Through his research on the desert, his work in the study and stewardship of wetlands, and in his leadership of his town of Dunn in developing a land stewardship program, Cal displays his passion for sharing the wonders of God's creation with other scientists, neighbors and citizens, religious leaders, and with professors and students of evangelical Christian colleges, universities and seminaries.

"In Christendom we need to recover a love for our Creator and a stewardship commitment to care for God's creation," Cal said, expressing his deep-seated and passionate conviction. Among the many results of his passion is Au

Sable Institute of Environmental Studies, an organization he helped found in 1979. Au Sable has developed into a program of service and Christian environmental stewardship to 60 evangelical colleges and universities over the past 27 years.

"I find it interesting that when nearly anyone—no matter what they believe—enters an untrammeled place in creation, they experience a sense of awe and wonder," he said. As for this witness given by God's creation, and by those who love God and care for creation, he advises Christians to move out into creation and immerse themselves in the beauty of the earth. "Part of our witness to Jesus Christ—as the one through whom God created, sustains and reconciles the whole creation (Colossians 1:15-20)—is for all of us to be willing, able, and eager to put ourselves, our children, our parents, neighbors, and others into the marvelous places across all of God's earth that instill in all of us the praise, joy, and wonder that wells up within us as human beings made in the image God—made to be in tune with God and with God's creation," he said.

"In my growing up, what I did quite unknowingly (because of my Christian home and community) was to learn and hold to the view that we learn about God, God's world, and God's will by reading two books—the Bible as the Book of God's Word and the creation as the Book of God's works. Many Sundays in church, while waiting for the service to begin, I read in the back of our worship book Article 2 of our *Confession of Faith* that described 'The Means by which We Know God:'

We know him by two means:

First, by the creation, preservation, and government of the universe,

since that universe is before our eyes like a beautiful
book
        in which all creatures,
        great and small,
        are as letters
        to make us ponder
        the invisible things of God:
        his eternal power
        and his divinity,
        as the apostle Paul says in Romans 1:20.

All these things are enough to convince men and leave
them without excuse.

Second, he makes himself known to us more openly
      by his holy and divine Word,
      as much as we need in this life,
      for his glory
      and for the salvation of his own.

"What do we learn from reading both books interactive-
ly and coherently? The short answer is that we learn everything we need to know to live rightly and to spread right living, and do this with passion and conviction because this is
what God requires of us; it is our joyful privilege and vocation.
"As we read both books coherently, we also come to
understand more fully what the Bible means as sin and sin-
fulness—of 'missing the mark.' We see this expressed in the
intended and unintended degrading and destruction of
God's creation (including people, of course). And we learn
from the Book of God's Word that we ought not participate in
or condone such degradation and destruction of the creation. This we find most explicitly summarized in two passages in the Book of God's Word, John 3:16 and Revelation

11:18. From the Bible we learn that believing on Jesus—the one through whom God created and sustains all things—brings everlasting life (John 3:16); also from the Bible we learn those who destroy the earth will themselves be destroyed. (Revelation 11:18) Taken together, we see clearly that believing and following Jesus is not compatible with actions or inactions that destroy the earth. To follow Jesus is to take care of creation.

"This is why I am so inspired by God's two books and why I am so dedicated to opposing earth's destruction and degradation. It is also the reason why I am so passionate about caring for God's creation—ourselves included—for this is a blessed, fulfilling, and fruitful privilege and responsibility."

CHAPTER THREE

The Environment:
The Great Omission

If thy heart were right, then every creature would be a mirror of life, and a book of holy doctrine. There is no creature so small and abject, but it reflects the goodness of God.

THOMAS A KEMPIS

The heavens tell of the glory of God. The skies display His marvelous craftsmanship.

PSALM 19:1

O nce while working to bring relief aid to the Karen people group in the mountains along the Burma-Thailand border, my wife Nancy and I were shocked by how fearful the Karen people were of us. Living in remote villages all their lives, these Burmese political and cultural refugees had never seen a white person. Whenever we would begin making our way through their villages, many of the people would scatter and run. Many times, the villages looked like ghost towns by the time we arrived.

As I began to learn more about the Karen people and the culture, I learned that they didn't believe in God as a person. They simply believed that everything—rocks, trees, water, etc.—had a spirit. They worshiped animals. They worshiped nature. At the time, I struggled to understand how I could share with them about a God they couldn't conceptualize who loved them so much. What could I say that would turn their heart toward the truth?

> For the truth about God is known to them instinctively. God has put this knowledge in their hearts. From the time the world was created, people have seen the earth and sky and all that God made. They can clearly see his invisible qualities – his eternal power and divine nature. So they have no excuse whatsoever for not knowing God.

> Yes, they knew God, but they wouldn't worship him as God or even give him thanks. And they began to think up foolish ideas of what God was like. The result was that their minds became dark and confused. Claiming to be wise, they became utter fools instead. And instead of worshiping the glorious,

ever-living God, they worshiped idols made to look like mere people, or birds and animals and snakes.

So God let them go ahead and do whatever shameful things their hearts desired. As a result, they did vile and degrading things with each other's bodies. Instead of believing what they knew was the truth about God, they deliberately chose to believe lies. So they worshiped the things God made but not the Creator Himself, who is to be praised forever. – Romans 1:19-25

Just like the people Paul wrote about in the first chapter of Romans, the Karen people were worshiping the things God made but not the Creator Himself. At the time I was working with the Karen people, had I been able to overlay the truth of the Gospel with God's heart for His creation, the Gospel would have been contextualized for these people! I never realized what an avenue I had. It was the creation that could have reached them. If we could take them past what was created to the One who created it, we would have been able to show them the truth.

THE NATURE OF THE GOSPEL

The heavens tell of the glory of God. The skies display His marvelous craftsmanship. Day after day they continue to speak; night after night they make him known. They speak without a sound or a word; their voice is silent in the skies; yet their message has gone out to all the earth, and their words to all the world. – Psalm 19:1-4

When I made a commitment to follow Jesus, almost immediately there was a desire in me to share with others the wonderful news of what He had done for me. I just had to tell anyone who would listen about the change that had started to take place in my life. So, naturally, I jumped at the chance when a friend of mine offered me an opportunity to smuggle Bibles into a Communist country.

After experiencing a transformation in my own soul, I was compelled to tell others. It's a God-given desire that wells up within all of us. It's intrinsic to our faith. And if it's truly alive within us, we cannot hide the Good News any more than nature can hide the splendor of God. When we discover the Kingdom of God, we realize that becoming a Christian is so much more than simply getting a ticket to heaven; living with the reality of the Kingdom in our hearts means that our lives are changed. Nothing is going to be the same again; not the way we view the world, not the way we make decisions, not the way we live our lives. My Christian journey is being shaped by seeing God's care for his creation. I want to participate with him, and it has begun to influence every aspect of my faith—including ways I can share the reality of the Kingdom of God. No longer can I view the environment as a political issue. Now it must become part of my faith, enveloped by the way I seek to live as a follower of Jesus.

The Kingdom of God is not something to be admired

> My Christian journey is being shaped by seeing God's care for his creation. I want to participate with him, and it has begun to influence every aspect of my faith.

from afar. It's something that must be lived—and shared. As I realize that environmental stewardship is part of true Kingdom living, the teaching that God cares for all creation and He has placed us to be stewards of it becomes not only part of something I believe; it becomes integrated into the way I live.

THE ENVIRONMENT AND THE GREAT COMMISSION

Just before Jesus ascended into heaven, His directive was clear:

> Therefore, go and make disciples of all the nations, baptizing them in the name of the Father and the Son and the Holy Spirit. Teach these new disciples to obey all the commands I have given you. And be sure of this: I am with you always, even to the end of the age. – Matthew 28:19-20

For years this statement has been labeled as the Great Commission, the responsibility of the church to share the truth of the Kingdom of God with others. As I understand it, this occurs in three ways. First, there is the proclamation, which is the assurance of God's existence and good news for mankind. Next, there is the demonstration of the Kingdom through signs and wonders, displaying God's heart for the world through acts of compassion and mercy through social justice. Finally, there is participation, which is discipleship, bringing people to become participants in biblical truth in life, obedience and stewardship. Discipleship is a verb that results in action. It's not just something in our head, but it goes to our hearts and hands, translating into a holistic sharing of

Christ's love with the world.

The more I study about God's call for us to steward His creation, the more convinced I am that it also rests perfectly within the confines of the Great Commission. Through becoming faithful stewards of creation, we are presented with an opportunity to share the Gospel. In becoming leaders in this area, we won't be selling out to a culturally compromised gospel; rather, we will be faithful in contextualizing the Gospel in our own nation as well as making it real for other people groups around the world.

As we bring the concept of environmental stewardship into conversation with the Great Commission, we see the synergy the two have. Let's take a look at how facets of the Great Commission merge with the practice of environmental stewardship.

Proclamation. When we think about it, we proclaim the Gospel in a number of ways. Some methods are more familiar to us than others. Primarily, we proclaim the Gospel by the sharing God's Word—and we share it as truth. We proclaim that the existence of God is evidenced through the written word and through the fulfillment of prophecies. In the early days, the proclamation of the Gospel was accomplished through the eyewitness testimony of the apostles, the men Jesus entrusted to building his church. In his first epistle, John writes that he saw everything prophesied about Jesus fulfilled. God's reality is also proclaimed through the evidence of the Holy Spirit transforming human lives today.

John Calvin wrote: "The creation is quite like a spacious and splendid house, provided and filled with the most exquisite and at the same time the most abundant furnishings. Everything in it tells us of God." As I shared earlier in the book, the proclamation of God's reality was made real to me through sitting in nature and admiring the beauty of the earth. It was through creation that I realized there must be a Creator behind it all. And that same realization is just begging to be proclaimed to animists in the mountains of Thailand and Burma. It's begging to be proclaimed to your neighbors across the street who constantly work on their garden every chance they get. It's begging to be proclaimed to the radical environmentalists who feel the urge to fight for creation but don't know why. But in many ways, the environment has been the neglected assurance of God's abundant presence.

In his book *Velvet Elvis,* Rob Bell shares a story that details just how compelling of a proclamation creation can be to some people who are desperately searching for God—and they don't even realize it. He was invited to officiate a wedding between two friends who told him they didn't want any mention of Jesus or God in the ceremony. However, the bride said, "Rob, do that thing you do. Make it really profound and deep and spiritual!" In a cabin in the middle of the woods, they began planning the ceremony. After Rob asked the couple why they had chosen this setting in nature for their ceremony, the groom said, "Something holds this all together."

Rob began a line of questioning that led the couple to come to a life-transforming conclusion: Whatever "force" that held nature together was the same force that brought them together as a couple. Eventually they decided that this "force" was what they would call "God." The idea that God was real began to resonate with this couple when someone pointed out that they enjoyed the peace and harmony in creation. Rob concluded his thoughts to readers, saying this couple is "closer to Jesus than they could ever imagine."

The assurance of God's existence is proclaimed all around us in His creation—and we shouldn't neglect it.

Demonstration. Why is it that when disaster strikes, the church is one of the first responders? Why do the poor turn to the church for help? The reason is simple: acts of compassion and mercy display the heart of God. This is especially true in the area of social injustice. Our desire to see justice take place is intrinsically linked to our relationship with God. He is a just God—and as participants in the Kingdom of God, we are to demonstrate acts of social justice, being an advocate for those who don't have a voice and aiding the helpless.

Consider these statistics:

• World Health Organization (WHO) reports that one in three people die prematurely or have disabilities because of poor nutrition and calorie deficiencies.

• The United Nations' Food and Agriculture Organization reports that more than 16,000 children die daily from hunger-related causes—one child every five seconds.

• WHO also reports that diarrhoeal disease is responsible for the deaths of 1.8 million people each year—and it's estimated that 88 percent of that burden is attributable to unsafe water supply, sanitation and hygiene and is mostly concentrated on children in developing countries.

• WHO estimates that three million people are killed worldwide by outdoor air pollution annually from vehicles and industrial emissions, 1.6 million indoors through using solid fuel. Most of these deaths happen in poor countries.

While these staggering statistics seem unfathomable for many in the Western world, they are the daily reality of many other people living in developing countries. And the root cause for many of these issues is environmental in nature, caused by misuse of land or lack of education in regards to sustainable living or sanitary practices.

How does going into a village in Ethiopia and drilling a well spread the love of Christ? It is a practical demonstration of the heart of God. We don't want these people to die, and they will if they don't have clean water. Caring for people in developing countries through means of environmental education and tools for them to continue to have a clean water supply is a way to practically show them God's love. Teaching people how to manage their land so they don't misuse it and extract all the nutrients out of it is also a way that helps us care for God's creation and demonstrate God's love. If they have food and proper nourishment, the people in developing countries will live longer and not die from so many malnourishment-related diseases.

In looking at the way we approach ministering to others through the lens of the Kingdom of God, we should follow Jesus' lead. He did not simply say, "be warm and be filled;" rather, he fed people and sent them home full. The demonstration of the Kingdom took place when the apostles cared for the widows and the orphans. Those acts of love and kindness spoke just as loudly as the signs and wonders that also demonstrated the heart of God. As followers of Jesus, we should be willing to help people in a practical way just as easily as we would pray for them and ask God to change them supernaturally.

Participation. The final aspect of the Great Commission is discipleship—to make disciples, obedient and willing participants in advancing the Kingdom of God. Discipleship is a verb, measured not so much by what we say but by what we do. In proclaiming the Good News to others and demonstrating the love of Christ in a practical way, we must fulfill the Great Commission by making disciples, teaching others in very practical ways how to follow Jesus.

As we begin to connect with people's hearts through sharing our love for God's creation, we will begin to have the opportunity to show people how to love the Creator. We model for others how a follower of Jesus pursues wholeness in relationship with God and other people. And we also model how we are to care for and steward what God has given us—whether it be our relationships, our money, our time, or our environment.

When we are presented with an idea such as changing people's views on the environment when they have been shaded by political overtones for decades, it can seem overwhelming. And when that happens, we have two choices: We could become paralyzed and do nothing. Or we can roll up our sleeves and get to work, taking a step forward, believing that God is leading us.

There are many people who talk about caring for the environment but are actually doing very little about it—so-called "environmentalists" included. I don't think you can proclaim something without doing something about it. The church has garnered a reputation for such inconsistent behavior, and we must begin to reverse that trend. This is not a topic that can simply be talked about. We must take the first step forward and follow where God leads us.

Ed Brown: Developing a new approach to missions

Ed Brown didn't hate the environment—he just had more important things to take care of, such as people's spiritual needs, student ministry, and evangelism. Caring for the environment was something he valued, but it didn't break into his high priority list ... until one day.

As Ed began to feel drawn toward missions, there was also a yearning to get involved with missions through the environment. "I realized that the missionary task in its most complete sense could not be carried out without including environmental issues as part of a strategic agenda," Ed said. "Many, if not most, of the problems being experienced in the developing world today are fundamentally caused by environmental abuses. If the damage being done to the environment is not addressed as part our relief efforts, we will not succeed in ministering to those in need, no matter how sincere our efforts.

"Thus I find myself compelled by my beliefs and convinced by practical realities. I reluctantly admit that I am an environmentalist."

Ed may be reluctant to admit it, but he is anything but a reluctant environmentalist. After serving as the CEO of the Au Sable Institute, an evangelical education and research program that offers hands-on training in environmental stewardship, he began to be drawn toward some type of environmental missions position—there just wasn't one available at the time.

"After working at Au Sable and being exposed to so much great information and teaching on environmental stewardship, I got the environmental bug," Ed said. "I began to learn what the real issues are in the world, and I wanted to help."

One of the real issues that Ed learned about what the rapid disappearance of forests in developing countries and how such a quick ecological transition can bring about climate shifts detrimental to the nation's survival. And as Ed entered into a transitional phase with his job at Au Sable, environmental missions found him in the form of Craig Sorley and Care of Creation.

"My position was ending because of organizational restructuring, and I was looking around wondering what I was going to do next," Ed said. "Craig heard I was going to be available and asked me to start a new organization with him. We took it bit by bit and we wrote up a plan that started circulating to various friends, and everyone began encouraging us to do this.

"The basic idea was to combine the environment and missions in a way we don't think anyone else is doing. On an organizational level, no mission organization in North America is openly both environmental and missional. It's very similar to medical missions in its approach to the mission field. When you take out the word 'medical' and put in the word 'environmental,' that's what we are. We want to do practical things where we help people by sharing the Gospel, but we want to serve people and serve the church by helping to heal the land through various means. In Kenya, this means reforestation."

Craig, whose educational background includes a forestry degree from the University of Minnesota, grew up as a missionary kid in Kenya and watched the forest disappear. He and his wife, Tracy, decided they wanted to go to Kenya and begin helping restore the forests. With sponsorship from the Sorleys' home church, John Piper's Bethlehem Baptist in Minneapolis, Craig and Tracy were ready to get to the field and needed Ed's help. It didn't take too long before Ed decided to partner with Craig and Tracy—and Care of Creation was born.

"Kenya is an interesting missions study," Ed said. "As a nation, it's about 80 percent Christian—and it could be looked at as a missionary success story. The churches are full, people read the Bible, and their own people pastor the churches. But at the same time the church has been exploding in Kenya, the people are worse off as far as their quality of life goes. They have poor water quality, the people are poor, the environment is collapsing, and their animals are dying at an alarming rate. It's primarily collapsing because of population pressure. The people don't know how to be good stewards of the land—and it's killing them.

"Our strategy looks like this: If Kenya is 80 percent Christian, then Christians are the best hope to reverse the trend in Kenya. If you can show them that God wants them to care for the environment and give them the tools to do so, it can change quickly."

While Ed wrestled with what it means to be a Christ-follower and truly care for the environment given today's political division over the topic, he has also had to battle the misgivings of other believers and mainstream Christian organizations that have no grid to process how caring for the environment is a value germane to Christian faith.

"One of the arguments I get into is the position that we need to care for people over the environment and that people are more important than plants and animals," he said. "My response is this: we, as people, depend on the environment to live. When the land goes bad for whatever reason, human life stops. You can't say people are more important than the land because it's a false dichotomy. When you care for the land, you're caring for the people. This is even more evident in a place like Kenya where people farm the land and live off it.

"In places like Kenya and Haiti, you find that environmental degradation creates a downward spiral of poverty. They use inappropriate farming techniques and have even less to live on than at first, and they become poor. We would like to see that reversed in Kenya."

Ed makes some pretty compelling cases when confronted by people who let their political tendencies prevent them from becoming people who care for God's creation.

"I've had to wrestle with this because I speak to some very conservative audiences," Ed said. "The initial response I get is, 'We can't be environmentalists because we're conservatives.' The heart of the evangelical faith and a great deal of what we believe as evangelicals is ecological. We believe God birthed creation, and we believe God has called us to take care of it."

Get involved with Care of Creation by visiting their website at: careofcreation.org

CHAPTER FOUR

How Faith and the Environment Merge

The initial step for a soul to come to knowledge of God is contemplation of nature.

IRENAEUS OF LYONS

Yours, O LORD, is the greatness, the power, the glory, the victory, and the majesty. Everything in the heavens and on earth is yours, O LORD, and this is your kingdom. We adore you as the one who is over all things.

1 CHRONICLES 29:11

A s our church began to wade into uncharted waters with our new environmental ministry, I was excited to see what would happen for a couple of reasons. For one, I wanted to see how the community would react to what we were doing. Would they ignore us? Question us? Make fun of us? Embrace us? The potential reactions were almost endless. The other reason I was excited about launching our new ministry was because I was curious to see how this new value in our church might open the door for members to share their faith with others. Would people question our motives? Inquire about our faith? Dismiss us as a gimmick church? Only time would tell if this was going to be an effective way to share the Gospel while we fulfilled the biblical mandate to care for God's creation.

It wasn't long before I received my answer. Stories began pouring into our staff about how leading our community in this value opened doors to conversations about Christ that never would have happened otherwise. One of my favorite stories happened when my administrative assistant, Lori, fielded a call from an environmental activist named Sam.

Sam had heard about our ministry to care for the environment and visited our website. Not knowing that we were a church, he called in to report his good environmental deed of the day—he was on his way to protest what some corporation was doing to the environment. After sharing this information with Lori, Sam awaited for some type of approval for what he was doing. But Lori didn't give it to him. Instead, she challenged him to move from protest to action.

"Sam, that's not the kind of thing we do here," Lori told him. "Instead of telling people what they're doing wrong all the time, we want to demonstrate how to do things right more than anything. We think we should care for the environment by being good stewards of it. If we do our part and help others understand how to care for the environment, then we can actually begin to change things." After a moment of contemplation, Sam replied, "That's what I believe, too." And the unsuspecting Sam was issued an invitation to church, which he warmly accepted.

MAKING THE CONNECTION

People in the mainstream media often misinterpret many Christians' actions. And if truth be told, they paint an accurate picture sometimes, too—and the truth is hard to swallow. However, no matter how Christians are depicted in the media, the one thing that will change people's perceptions about Christians is knowing one personally who is living out a faith that saturates every part of that person's life. There are always areas that we can improve upon, but when God begins prompting wholesale change, we cannot ignore Him. The environment is one such issue that for too long has gone largely ignored by many Christians—and this hasn't been misinterpreted by anyone.

Reversing those perceptions is as simple—and yet, as complicated—as applying true repentance to our lives: we stop moving in one direction and begin moving in the opposite direction. Instead of ignoring the environment, we become the leaders in caring for God's creation. It will earn you a puzzled look highlighted by a furrowed brow. "But you're a Christian," they might protest. "You don't care about the environment." However, they're only half right, and you must readjust their perception—"No, I am a Christian; therefore, I do care about the environment."

As our actions begin to back up our talk, the world will begin to see a clearer picture emerge about what it means to follow God. Our deeds will speak so much more than our words. We've all heard the saying, "People don't care how much you know, until they know how much you care." The church can quickly become the leader in this area because many environmental groups merely express a love for God's creation without doing much about it.

SHARING CHRIST IN YOUR CITY

Let's face it: most Christians are scared to share their faith because of what might happen. "Will they ask a question I can't answer? What if I don't know how to respond? What if they laugh at me?" We can think of lists a mile long of reasons not to talk about our faith with other people. But when we feel most comfortable—and excited about what God is doing within us—is when someone asks us about our faith. Instead of trying to find some clever way to start the conversation (which Jesus didn't do either, by the way—He was merely being who He was), the other person starts the conversation, and we get to simply tell about our faith.

While Christian t-shirts rarely spark a favorable response or line of questioning from other people, our reusable "green bags" (canvas bags used for shopping which eliminates the need for plastic bags) create a curiosity that people just can't handle. They have to ask about the bags. "Where did you get those bags?" the stranger asks. "From my church," is the surprising response. "Really? Your church sells those? Why?" fires off the inquiring mind. "Well, because we believe in being good stewards of the environment—and cutting down on the number of plastic or paper bags is one way to do that," is the stunning rejoinder. (However, recycling plastic bags you get at the grocery store is also a good way to be friendly to the environment. Many stores will take your old plastic bags—and some will even pay a small amount for each bag.)

Before you can say "paper or plastic," the questions start coming. Suddenly, an unsuspecting grocery shopper is arrested by the thought that a church in their city just might actually care about God's creation as much as the shopper does. In Boise, a city that is known for its endless outdoor activities, people hold the environment as an important value, even though they may not be doing much about it themselves. So especially in our town, when people start seeing the church take the lead in caring for the environment, they are intrigued. And for some, the church's lack of respect for the environment might be the reason why they always dismissed the idea of becoming part of a church community.

> I have found that upholding the value of stewardship of God's creation in your community can also create unsuspecting opportunities for evangelism.

I am a firm believer in sharing the love of Christ through practical demonstrations. Feeding the poor, repairing someone's home or handing out free juice on a hot day are all examples of servant evangelism. Likewise, I have found that upholding the value of stewardship of God's creation in your community can also create unsuspecting opportunities for evangelism. I was most surprised by an idea our staff came up with in the way that it has generated so many opportunities for people in our church to share their faith.

After seeing the devastation of hurricane Katrina in New Orleans, we wanted to create opportunities for people to assist first-hand in rebuilding the city. One of our retired members volunteered to take his motor home down to New Orleans and lead weekly projects in the city. Our only obstacle was funding. So, in an effort to merge two values together—the value of stewardship over God's creation and the value of caring for people—our staff developed an outreach event that was wildly successful. We created paper bags that could be hung on the door handle of a home, which included a note explaining that we were collecting old cell phones for recycling and would return at a certain time to collect them. The note also shared how the funds raised from the cell phones would go toward helping our relief aid to Katrina victims in the New Orleans area. Also included in the bags was an article about our church's approach to environmental stewardship and why this was such an important value for us.

The response didn't surprise me. Americans are so generous when disaster strikes, especially when it hits their own people. But what did surprise me were the stories I heard from those who returned to homes to collect the cell phones. People weren't simply handing over their phones—they had questions, such as why would a church care about the environment so much. It gave our members opportunities to share the reality of their faith, explaining that it wasn't simply something they believed but something they lived. In the past, we have received good responses from people when we gave them things, but allowing others to participate in what we were doing stimulated the best responses we've ever had.

From the moment we began promoting and modeling caring for God's creation as a value in our church, there has always been such enthusiasm by our people and favor within the community. Someone donated a billboard to us. Someone else gave us a box truck that we painted our environmental ministry logo on the side and used it to transport recyclable goods to a local recycling facility. Throughout all the time I've spent in full-time ministry, I've started many ministries, but I've rarely seen the supernatural hand of God make things happen like He has with this particular project. I've seen ministries hit the wall and not go anywhere. And then I've seen some ministries take on a life of their own—our environmental stewardship ministry falls into that category. The only thing I can attribute this to is that God really approves of what we are doing. He likes the fact that we are willing to step out and break status quo, taking a huge risk to tend His garden.

SHARING CHRIST ABROAD

Caring for the environment opens so many doors on so many levels to take the love of Christ to others around the world. And caring for the earth is a crucial building block for us to show how much we, as Christians, love people. I have heard plenty of arguments that claim we should care for people above all else—and I agree. However, caring for people is not at odds with being good stewards of the earth. In fact, they go hand in hand. Caring for the environment is a powerful way for us to show that we care about people.

In the previous chapter, we discussed the issues surrounding unsanitary water in developing nations. As a result of learning about this environmental hazard, our mission teams began digging wells in the resettlement villages throughout the Philippines. There are also return trips planned where these teams will install solar pumps that will help keep the water even cleaner and more readily accessible to the people. As Christians, we are compelled to help the helpless. If we know a solution to the problem causing so much disease, aren't we obligated to help correct it? Sending mission team after mission team to help sick people in areas that have no clean water is one way the church has chosen to approach the problem. However, I believe we must also be willing to address the bigger issue of contaminated water by helping dig wells that will result in clean, healthy living for people in developing nations.

Consider this staggering observation: Contaminated land is a problem in industrialized countries, but it is also a problem in developing countries where pesticides and nitrate-rich fertilizers damage the environment. When the land becomes infertile in a developing country, starvation is sure to follow. With such rampant poverty in some of these countries, a problem of this magnitude can seem insurmountable and lead to much hopelessness.

Sir John Houghton, one of the world's leading environmental scientists, recently explained how caring for the environment in developing countries equates to truly caring for people: "Aid and debt relief are not the end of the story for Africa. Climate change will increase the continent's problems very seriously, and already has. What is the point of taking steps to reduce poverty with one hand while, by ignoring climate change, increasing it with the other? The two problems are inseparable."

That is why caring for the environment can become one

of the most powerful tools for evangelism in the 21st Century. We can—and should—care for the sick as much as possible. But there will be far fewer sick people to help when the environment becomes more livable, through means such as clean water and nutrient-rich soil. Through caring for the environment, the church will be afforded access to areas that at one time were closed to Christians, much like medical missions opened many doors during the 20th Century.

However, we must take it one step farther and educate people on the dangers to their natural resources, equipping them with the knowledge to renew them and protect them from contaminants. In Rick Warren's Global PEACE Plan, he outlines five areas of how we can help developing countries deal with both spiritual disease (**P**lant churches and **E**quip servant leaders) and physical disease (**A**ssist the poor, **C**are for the sick, and **E**ducate the next generation). He understands how important education is to ensuring that all the work they do lasts, much like Jesus saw discipleship was important to continuing to promote the Gospel. The element of education is what prevents a recurring pattern from taking place in these countries—this must co-exist with the church's efforts to help restore an environmental harmony that will empower and equip people to become good stewards of God's creation.

Warren was also among a group of evangelical leaders to endorse the Evangelical Climate Initiative's "Climate Change: An Evangelical Call to Action." This position paper states that Christians are obligated to respond to the climate change problem due to moral convictions—and it asks governments, businesses, churches and individuals to consider the role they might play in this issue. Both at home and abroad, ecological disaster stands as an issue that we must face and lead.

SHARING CHRIST IN DISASTER

One of the greatest debates today deals with the issues that surround global warming. Volatile discussions on this subject have been added to a long list of world crisis topics that have polarized people into opposing camps. For the Christian who desires to be informed on global environmental concerns, it is becoming increasingly difficult not to join forces with one side or the other. When the Lord first prompted me to develop an environmental ministry at our church, I had a strong conviction to keep it free from political bias, which has been a great challenge due to the fact it is a milieu highly charged with the polarities of politics. As Christians we must be discerning and view the world's problems as they truly are, weighing them against biblical truth in sensitive ways rather than joining in knee-jerk social reaction.

The truth is, our planet is heating up, and the facts are rapidly becoming indisputable. The temperature of the sea is raising, glacier ice is receding, and the world's climate is changing. This warming trend is not only affecting ecosystems but is also clearly increasing hurricane activity and intensity. The focus of the global warming debate isn't so much centered on whether the earth's oceans and atmosphere are warming but rather why the phenomenon is taking place now. Is it something caused by human influence or simply the result of natural weather cycles? One camp emphatically claims that global warming has occurred due to the misuse and overuse of fossil fuels, which have been creating a greenhouse effect, trapping warm air beneath the earth's atmosphere. The other camp denies this accusation, claiming that what is alleged to be scientific fact is a mere hypothesis. They also cite historical weather records and trends to prove that the earth has always gone through climatic cycles and the present warming trend is just one of those cycles. But regardless of what your conclusion may be, the earth is currently in an indisputable warming trend.

For the Christian who cares about the earth and humanity, it is essential that we don't put our head in the sand on this very crucial phenomenon. No matter what has caused the earth's temperature to elevate, the result is hurting creation and devastating people's lives. For those of us who spent time helping in the clean up of the destructive Gulf Coast hurricanes of 2005, the reality of the matter became very evident. In our nation's history, hurricanes Katrina and Rita have caused humanitarian disasters in certain cities equaled only by the 1930s' Great Depression. This is to say nothing of the devastating tsunami that occurred as a result of an earthquake in the Indian Ocean or the record high summer temperatures in France in 2003, which caused nearly 15,000 heat-related deaths (mostly among the elderly) and are attributed by many to global climate change of a kind that Europe was simply unprepared for.

The manifestation of the warming of the Gulf of Mexico has made many Christians aware of the need, causing them to prepare to meet new and increasing demands for humanitarian aid in order to minister in compassion and mercy. Like never before in recent history, the church must rise to the occasion for humanitarian service. It is not an hour for the church to remain lethargic or silent. As we look to the future, the church must be prepared for such disasters and become the beacon of hope that God has called us to be in what can be a very dark world at times.

Whether it is in the daily grind, through exciting adventures overseas, or in the midst of catastrophic natural disasters, the church needs to be leading the way in caring for people and the environment. By caring for God's creation on a daily basis, we can show our neighbors what it means to be a good steward of what God has given you. By caring for God's creation overseas, we can show people from other nations how to be good stewards of what God has given them. By caring for God's people following natural disasters, we can show people cleaning up a neighborhood in a responsible way and meeting people's needs in maybe the darkest time in their lives share the love of Christ in the most practical of ways. After we do these things, people will listen to what we have to say when it comes to our relationship with God.

Peter Illyn:
The Environmental Evangelist

Peter Illyn always knew there was something special about being in nature. But it took a four-month, 1,000-mile trek with two llamas through the Cascades to discover just what was so special about it. And Illyn, who served for nine years as a pastor in Oregon and Washington, began to be drawn in another direction after his trip through the Cascades.

"I was wired for caring for the environment long before I entered the ministry," Illyn said. "While I was in ministry, I was constantly taking young folks out hiking to experience the grandeur and splendor of God's creation. Deep down, I believe God made a good earth and I am called to be a good steward and protect the fruitfulness and connectedness of creation."

In the book *Sacred Pathways*, author Gary Thomas describes nine different ways people really connect with God, and Thomas's description of a "naturalist" really hit home for Illyn. "I feel like I am a naturalist in the sense that the book describes it. Within Christendom and particularly in the evangelical world today, there have always been people who were nature lovers. But during my trek through the Cascades, I began to see the earth not only needs to be enjoyed, but protected as well so others can enjoy it, too. I was quite unaware of environmental issues until I came out of the woods and saw the fights in the Northwest over the logging of ancient forests and protecting endangered species like salmon and spotted owls."

Now, Illyn leads an environmental parachurch ministry called Restoring Eden, opening doors for him to speak at college campuses and churches across the country on why

Christians should care for the environment and how they can do so. Though he recognizes the church has not been overtly hostile toward environmental issues, the church's silence and apathy has been damaging.

"While the church has not attacked the environment, there has been this idea that caring for the earth is unnecessary and that it is a slippery slope to earth worshipping," Illyn said. "Many Christians I talk to think that being an environmentalist means that you have to be radical in your approach. This is not the case. For example, while I am pro-life when it comes to the issue of abortion, my views aren't represented by some self-righteous lunatic who bombs abortion clinics. When it comes to the environment, I don't have to be extremist either—just balanced in my approach."

Illyn has found that the major roadblock for evangelicals is the polarized political landscape that forces people into making a decision between only two choices—human life or the environment. "Politics create this disconnect for people in the U.S., whether they are Christians or otherwise," he said. "We are presented with false choices all the time, meaning we have to choose between two things that we shouldn't have to choose between.

"In a conversation I had with a pastor, he was connecting with this idea of environmental stewardship on so many levels. But when it came time to ask him if he would lead his church in getting involved, he said, 'I'm not ready to live in a grass hut with no electricity.' He created this false choice that caring for the earth meant we had to live in grass huts with no electricity. Politicians create these false choices all the time, but so does the church, sometimes making it 'us versus them.' Some evangelical leaders try to make it sound like if you're loving and serving the earth, then somehow you're not loving and serving God. We just need bigger hearts. For me, my faith is made stronger by my care for the earth. And in return, my care for the earth is giving me life because of my love for God, the Creator."

Illyn elicits many different responses from the Christians who hear his talks. One such response is captured by the western world's ability to compartmentalize its thinking, according to Illyn. "Having a compartmentalized worldview hurts Christians in so many ways," he said. "We can tell everyone we're pro-life all we want, but being consistently pro-life has just as much to do with government policy allowing abortion as it does about government policy allowing destructive material to go into the environment that kills a child from Texas with a condition he contracted while playing outside. Some aspects are just easier to get your hands around than others. We can't separate one from another just because it's convenient."

While Restoring Eden is more focused on awareness and urging people to take action through caring for creation where they live, Illyn also ventures into an area that makes many people nervous—public advocacy.

"As I entered into this debate with a heart for seeing God's creation restored, I felt called to become more than just someone who was sympathetic toward the environmental movement," Illyn said. "There was at a point where I started stepping over and into political activism. There are times when our voice has to be heard in the public arena. Usually we can get a solid consensus that God made a good earth and we're supposed to be a good steward of it, but when we start saying what stewardship looks like for people, then it gets tough. And when you say you support laws that protect the long-term health of the environment that are pitted against short-term economic concerns, people are ready to leave.

"But what I've found is that we need to talk about this so we don't have all these misunderstandings. The young college environmental activist who has never worked a day in his life wants to prevent the forests from being logged, while the logger just wants to make a living. Both of them have noble intentions, but there has to be a way to find a solution that sustains economic growth yet keeps the environment clean and healthy. That's what we can do by entering these environmental debates."

Illyn says that there are many ways to get involved in the politics of the environment, however, without ever marching around with a picket sign.

"One of the ways people can get involved politically is through the act of writing letters to public officials," Illyn said. "You can write letters to the editor of your newspaper. But more importantly you need to tell the leaders in Washington that environmental stewardship matters. The act of letter writing or calling government officials to let your opinion be heard is vital. Congressional delegates sometimes decide their votes by as little as 5-10 contacts from constituents. The fact that we're Christians and we don't see the world in "either/or" terms is profoundly refreshing for elected officials. It can allow them to vote their conscience instead of voting straight party lines.

"Also, people can look for opportunities to serve on resource planning committees. Not all environmental issues are national or controversial. Many environmental issues happen on a local level. And always be mindful that your dollar counts—the political arena is affected the market, which sometimes drives the policy that is being developed."

Ultimately, Illyn wants to see Christians grasp how important it is to care for creation and then to do something about it. "I remind people that there is no other place in the universe that supports life the way our planet does," he said. "The laws of nature are themselves a miracle. The same ingredients we breathe out are necessary for plants to live, so they can produce oxygen. ... We've got this amazing cycle of life, the earth is tilted just right, and we have these four seasons. Every creationist in my mind should also be an environmentalist or a conservationist because when we look around and see what an awesome world we live in, we should do what we can to help it be that much more fruitful."

Visit Peter's website at www.restoringeden.org.

CHAPTER FIVE

The Ripple Effect of Environmental Stewardship

We cannot be excused when we have not at all considered God in His works. He does not at all leave Himself without witness here. ... Let us then only open our eyes and we will have enough arguments for the grandeur of God, so that we may learn to honor Him as He deserves.

JOHN CALVIN

All creation anticipates the day when it will join God's children in glorious freedom from death and decay. For we know that all creation has been groaning as in the pains of childbirth right up to the present time.

ROMANS 8:21-22

Looking out over a glassy body of water, it's almost irresistible. In fact, you have probably been there at one point, too, standing on the bank of a calm lake or pond and fighting the urge. Eventually, you can't take it any more. The water just looks too smooth to be uninterrupted. So, you reach down and pick up a small stone before launching it over the water. When it finally splashes down with a solid ker-plunk, the waves begin to ripple out until the quiet undisturbed water at your feet laps upon the bank. The water has been stirred.

Life-changing moments are usually anything but a moment. When God does something so profound in our lives that it compels us to give Him all our attention, the "moment" is merely the culmination of what has been brewing beneath the surface for quite some time. For most people, the day after saying a prayer and committing their life to God does not result in an outward, immediate life transformation. Instead, transformation is what occurs over a period of time when one is committed to a central theme or idea—or in a Christian's case, committed to God.

WAVES OF CONSEQUENCE

Many people today believe that their actions don't harm anyone but themselves. They can't understand how what they do affects others. And while Christians seem to grasp this concept on some level, especially as it relates to sin in our lives, we don't always connect with the idea that our actions affect more than just other people.

Consider Paul's words regarding creation and its reaction to human actions:

For all creation is waiting eagerly for that future day when God will reveal who His children really are. Against its will, everything on earth was subjected to God's curse. All creation anticipates the day when it will join God's children in glorious freedom from death and decay. For we know that all creation has been groaning as in the pains of childbirth right up to the present time. And even we Christians, although we have the Holy Spirit within us as a fore-taste of future glory, also groan to be released from pain and suffering. We, too, wait anxiously for that day when God will give us our full rights as His children, including the new bodies He has promised us. Now that we are saved, we eagerly look forward to this freedom. For if you already have something, you don't need to hope for it. But if we look forward to something we don't have yet, we must wait patiently and confidently. — Romans 8:19-25

Just like mankind, creation was placed in bondage due to sin. Creation "has been groaning" because everything changed. No longer was there an easy life in a glorious garden. Now, it was hard work and sweat that would sustain life—and that didn't just go for us; rather, this bondage extended to all of creation. God's purpose and design was for us to live in freedom, in personal and intimate relationship with Him. But sin altered that design—and it was up to God to restore His original intent and purpose.

Through the death and resurrection of Jesus, God brought back freedom, beginning the restoration process of His creation with people. Just like we haven't seen the fullness of God's restoration power in our own lives—merely shades of it and flashes here and there—we haven't seen the fullness of God's restoration with the rest of creation. And just like God uses us to participate in His plan of redemption in the lives of others, God wants to use us in redeeming His creation and becoming good stewards of it. But we cannot expect to make a big splash and change everything instantly. The first splash must be within our own hearts.

The whole idea of environmental stewardship relates directly to the ripple effect. It starts near and goes far. There is a splash that begins everything—and it slowly begins to permeate every aspect of our lives. Instead of containing the splash and compartmentalizing it, we allow its waves to flow freely and change us from the inside out.

When Jesus was preparing to ascend into heaven, He told His disciples to gather in Jerusalem and wait for the Holy Spirit to empower them. As Peter and the other disciples had painfully experienced, no matter how much they loved Jesus, they could not walk out the life they were called to lead on their own strength. They needed something more than steely resolve. They needed the Holy Spirit. And "everyone present was filled with the Holy Spirit" (Acts 2:4a). That was the splash that began to resonate in their hearts and extend beyond. The Holy Spirits' effect was seen almost immediately through Peter, a man who just a few weeks before had denied knowing Jesus but was now delivering a stirring message that moved people to devote their lives to God.

This powerful moment began to build a holy momentum through people allowing this experience to be more than just an experience. Instead of the disciples fondly recalling the day the Holy Spirit displayed His power openly, they began to rely on the Spirit's power to become the kind of people Jesus had called them to be. And they couldn't stop telling others about it either. This experience started near to them and eventually reached far.

Any idea that is going to challenge people and change lives beyond ourselves must first take root in our own hearts. We cannot try to change the world when we have not been changed ourselves. When we speak of environmental stewardship, we have to understand that any change that is ever going to happen in the world around us starts with that sudden impact in our own hearts.

> Any idea that is going to challenge people and change lives beyond ourselves must first take root in our own hearts.

One of the themes of Romans 8 is that all creation is affected by humanity's freedom from bondage. The opposite of that is that all people are affected by humanity's sin. It not only affected the hearts of mankind, it also affected all of creation. Paul says our sin affects everything around us—our bodies, our minds, our relationships and ultimately God's creation all around us. There was a ripple effect started here. But if anything is going to ever change, it must flow outward in its proper order.

SEVEN RIPPLES OF CHANGE

In our desire to see God transform us, we must understand seven ripples of transformation and note how they impact our lives.

The first ripple that impacts our lives is in our hearts.

The first question that we must ask is what is the "environmental condition" of our hearts? Is there pollution and contamination that needs to be purified? We have to ask ourselves, "What is in our hearts?" Christ came to bring wholeness and purity to the broken and empty. In Mark 12, Jesus shares with us the greatest commandment: "And you must love the Lord your God with all your heart, all your soul, all your mind, and all your strength" (v. 30).

It begins with the heart, where we come to realize the impact of what happens there and how it affects our actions. Jesus came so that our heart might be healed and that our sin might be forgiven, that the contamination of our lives before we entered into a relationship with Jesus would go away and we would be purified. It begins through this relationship with Christ, and the revelation that we're not on this earth by accident but that God intended us to be here. And we're not just here, but we're here *right now*. We're here to make an impact. With that comes the incredible miracle of rebirth whereby we don't let the past paralyze us.

How often do we watch the news and hear about someone who is on a crusade to change the world around them and we hear their motivating impetus as one of anger, not love? We then realize that this is not a righteous cause. They are trying to make an impact by splashing on the banks, causing waves that will never change anything. The first ripple begins in our own hearts—and from there, everything else emerges.

Once our hearts have been impacted, the second ripple that affects us in our minds. The heart impacts the environmental condition of our mind—and the ripple continues. We have to ask ourselves these questions: Is there anything that is polluting my mind? Is anything polluting my thought life? Maybe my mind is being contaminated by resentment, jealousy, rage, or anger? Maybe pornography or other unrighteous thoughts?

In Romans 12:2, Paul writes, "Don't copy the behavior and customs of this world, but let God transform you into a new person by changing the way you think. Then you will know what God wants you to do, and you will know how good and pleasing and perfect His will really is." Our whole paradigm is changed through the love of God in our hearts. After this transformation, we begin to understand what it is that God wants to do with us and how He wants us to conduct ourselves in the world He has given us.

The next ripple that impacts us is our body. The condition of our mind impacts how we care for our body. And we have to ask ourselves these questions: Am I a good steward of my body? Or do I abuse it and misuse it? For many people who misuse their body, it relates back to having a wrong view of how God sees them. The purpose of the body is to sustain us and carry us through this life so we can do God's will.

The thing we must remember through this process is that God has given us a body and called us to be a good steward of it. It's God's gift to us. But some people have a twisted view of their body. They pollute their bodies with drugs or alcohol abuse, or they deprive it of the nutritious food it needs to function properly. When their bodies don't function properly, many times it is because of how they have abused it. Oftentimes, this abuse relates back to how they view themselves, believing they only have life to live for themselves.

My wife Nancy reminds me all the time that my body is not my own. In fact, she helps me steward my body. While I enjoy wide-open adventure, she enjoys her husband in one piece. She reminds me to be safe on tall ladders (or don't climb them altogether) and avoid riding bucking horses. She gives me massive amounts of vitamins and cooks healthy meals for us. When we understand that our body is not our own, we realize that we have a new responsibility—a responsibility to God and others. It changes the way we see ourselves.

The fourth ripple flows into our homes. Once change begins to take root in our hearts and trickle down to our minds and body, we have some more questions to ask ourselves: Am I tending the garden of my home or am I allowing weeds to grow? Is something polluting my home? My marriage? My kids? Or is life being sown into them?

Whether there is frustration or silence, when things are not right at home, nothing can really be right beyond the home. We cannot ignore what happens there on our watch. We have to monitor what our children watch on TV, just as much as we have to be careful about what we watch. We have to consider issues of neglect, anger and fear. We have to determine to have a good environment in our homes and take responsibility for it. Once this begins, we begin to see the physical environment in which we live in a new light. There is something about having a clean home, devoid of complete disarray—it speaks of peace and someone who is trying to be a good steward.

Also in our homes, we realize how parenting affects the landscape—both in a figurative and literal sense. In a figurative sense, how we raise our kids determines what kind of impact and influence they will have as they enter the world as adults. In a literal sense, how we raise our kids can directly affect the land. When the Lord was speaking through

Malachi, he said, "Look, I am sending you the prophet Elijah before the great and dreadful day of the Lord arrives. His preaching will turn the hearts of parents to their children, and the hearts of children to their parents. Otherwise I will come and strike the land with a curse" (Malachi 4:5-6).

It's so important for us to train our kids with solid Christian values, enabling these impacting ideals to flow from their hearts and into the world. And environmental stewardship is an integral part of this, something we must endeavor to impart to our children. In our church, one of the ways I have encouraged families to raise the value of God's creation within our families was to set up an art gallery full of images of families out enjoying nature. We asked people to bring in pictures of their families out in creation. If they didn't have any, this was the call to get out and enjoy nature! If we have never been exposed to the beauty of God's creation, we will never fully appreciate it. This helped raise the value of environmental stewardship in the homes of our congregation as it had already begun to hit home in their hearts, minds, and bodies.

There are consequences for everything we do—and when we are following the way Jesus has called us to live, then the consequences will be ones that help establish the Kingdom of God in the hearts of people. What we do in our homes flows far beyond the walls of our houses. It pours out through the lives of all those who live there, including ourselves.

The fifth ripple impacts the church. When we realize that the church has veered off its original course, deviating from its intended purpose and design, we must be willing to make a change. With all the different voices that influence the church, it's easy to see how she can get distracted from what

Jesus intended her to be. But more often than not, it's the people who have been impacted in the hearts, minds, bodies, and homes that carry powerful, passionate messages to the church. When the church hears these messages, something begins to stir—both on an individual level and on a corporate level.

The kind of environment the early church sought to develop was one where the people were in one heart and mind with one another—they were together in one faith in Jesus. If we can't get along with people who have the same heart and mind, how are we going to get along with people who don't share all our same values? Being a good environmentalist means that we create a good environment around us. We do that when God's impact on our hearts, minds, and homes is free to operate in the larger household of faith.

The church is a powerful vehicle capable of bringing about change in our neighborhoods as well as our nation when motivated through our love for Jesus. The Body of Christ calls us to participate in something far greater than ourselves, as the Holy Spirit equips us with the opportunity to do so. Instead of a stale institution, the corporate church needs to be an organic representation of what is actually occurring in the hearts of people. When we reach out to others with giving hearts full of love and mercy, we are an expression of God's love for people—a people who understand God's nature of mercy and grace toward us and want to give that same heart toward others. And we create an environment that allows God's love to heal the broken and hurting. But the ripple doesn't stop there.

Next, the ripple hits our communities and neighborhoods. In explaining the second greatest commandment,

Jesus says, "Love your neighbor as yourself" (Mark 12:31). We are bringing the love of God to the streets, not necessarily in words, but in our actions and attitudes. If we love our neighbors, we mow our lawn and paint our houses out of respect for them. We try to show love in practical ways. We may also care for them in other ways as well, bringing them meals when they are sick or just had a baby. Of course, many of us have to take the step to meet our neighbors first! The change that once began in our hearts and church is now emanating in a very tangible way.

Now this ripple is beginning to play out into a literal physical environment as it reaches beyond us. If it hasn't happened in our hearts and minds, we are bound. And if we are bound, we cannot reach out. Christ came to release our hands and our feet so we might love our neighbor as ourselves. Self love may sound egotistical; however, self love is really simply understanding how much you are loved. It's healing.

> Christ came to release our hands and our feet so we might love our neighbor as ourselves.

Without it, you cannot love your neighbor. We can only love because God's love for us gives us an understanding of the gift he has given us.

Finally, the ripple reaches its final point of impact— the world. We look beyond ourselves and we become aware of the gift of creation. We thank God for what He has done. We appreciate his handiwork on a new level—and we want to join in helping the Lord restore it.

God began this work by moving us at our core—He started with our heart. Then, we asked him to get all the contaminants out of our mind. We followed that by asking God to help us take better care of our body. From there, we wanted to get the environment right in our homes—and then to be a good participant in getting it right in our neighborhood. Then, we began to see the bigger picture, the one that included us making a difference in the world.

If we don't deal with our heart first, creation will groan. Environmental stewardship starts in the heart and in our inner places as we let God do His work in our lives, so we might leave the world a better place from our time on this earth.

Dr. Paul Rothrock:
Changing Minds One Class at a Time

At the start of each school year when Dr. Paul Rothrock is preparing for the next incoming class at Taylor University to take his Environment and Society course, he knows he is not preaching to the choir. Unlike most secular colleges and universities where the idea of caring for the environment is en vogue, Rothrock's classes are composed of students who usually come from strong Christian homes—and places where environmental stewardship is not usually a high priority.

"I think many of the students are surprised at the content and how informative and interesting it really is," said Rothrock, whose university turned out EPA Administrator, Stephen L. Johnson. "I think there's some sense that they should be on their guard as they begin. But generally the class seems to have a pretty good response as they go through it."

As Rothrock begins his class each semester, what he finds through loose surveys are in line with the general attitude of Christians toward the environment.

"I start the class with just the question of how many are environmentalists," Rothrock said. "Over the years, I don't think I've ever gotten more than 15 percent of the people in the class to give a positive response to that. Often it's this kind of blank look, and then I even try to encourage them to give a positive response. Then someone may ask what we mean by 'environmentalism,' but I don't like to answer them. I want to let them play with that in their mind and figure out what it means. People think environmentalism is a tree hugger or a recycler. They have a very naïve idea of what environmentalism is as they start the class. And to the extent that they've heard about it, it's got a negative stereotype to it, which is why not many of the students admit that they are environmentalists."

By being afforded the opportunity to teach aspects of environmental stewardship through the lens of Christian faith, Rothrock is able to lay a foundation that makes sense for the students. In their first lab, the students are given a Bible study that has verses pertaining to the environment and are asked to respond to questions about the text.

"We don't do this to preach to them but to bring them to an awareness and get them to interact with those passages," Rothrock said. "We touch on those passages at the end of the semester in two different ways. We think about all the different ethical perspectives and what are the scriptural relationships between them. The students also discover that there are different scriptural perspectives as well—and there's not a monolithic answer. There's not a necessity for there to be an ethnocentric answer as well. The general public is quite surprised when Christians see the importance of doing something that's just better for people. But there are scriptural viewpoints that go beyond that in explaining why we need to be good stewards of the earth God has given us."

Rothrock, who didn't grow up in an evangelical Christian home, said his family discussed environmental issues and had a strong conservation ethic and an appreciation for nature. So, when he followed his passions and began studying biology, he approached it with a natural favor toward the environmental connection. But not growing up in a Christian home has given him a perspective to the topic that is beneficial in getting his students to connect the idea of environmentalism with their faith, especially when it comes to sharing one's faith.

"I think environmental issues helps us find another point of unity to work with people of different persuasions,"

Rothrock said. "On the last day of the class, we look at a handout that I suggest they could use as a small group guide to talk about some of these issues. It pulls out a couple of things from the course and reviews some of the stewardship passages. It ends with asking a few lifestyle questions and trying to get people to consider a little bit of the American style of materialism that is very much prevalent in the church here. In one of our labs that's entitled 'Afluenza,' we examine the impact of consumerism on people—and it connects very directly to environmentalism. It encourages an examination of lifestyle. It's one of the things they learn here and it's very shocking."

In showing other believers how environmental stewardship needs to become a value in their lives, Rothrock said there are obstacles people face, including many of the same ones he runs up against with his students. "I think the environment is not identified as a conservative issue, and most evangelical Christians would identify with being conservative in their political views," he said. "The environmental issues tend to be identified with being 'New Age.' Also, life science and biology are related topics connected with evolution—thus many Christians have a negative attitude toward science. There's a lot of baggage that's brought into these discussions."

Nevertheless, Rothrock wants to do his part in exposing young Christian adults to environmental stewardship that hopefully challenges them to look at the way they live and consider how it could be even more in line with a true biblical worldview.

"I try to leave them with the notion that whatever you want to call it, it's still part of our heritage as Christians," Rothrock said. "And I don't want to let the stereotypes of environmentalists detract from their willingness to pursue these ideas. Also, I like to point out that this is a ministry opportunity that is often ignored. There's no good reason why we couldn't work with people of all sorts of belief systems. I think that's what our calling should be. I think that's a place where we can be supportive of what unbelievers are doing. We impress others when they can see that we can go along with what they're doing—and we're doing it because we believe it's the right thing to do, even if our reasons vary from theirs."

Visit www.taylor.edu to learn more about the school's Earth and Environmental Sciences Department.

CHAPTER SIX

Noah:
Man of Action

We can gather that all the creatures of the world lead the mind of the contemplative and wise man to the eternal God. For these creatures are shadows, echoes and pictures ... and vestiges proposed to us and signs divinely given so that we can see God.

ST. BONAVENTURE

O Lord, what a variety of things you have made! In wisdom you have made them all. The earth is full of your creatures.

PSALM 104:24

S ometimes big visions call for small steps. While you may dream the grandest of dreams, nothing puts you on the path toward accomplishing them except the first step. Likewise, when God plants a dream in your heart, the process toward bringing that dream to fruition starts through simple obedience by doing what He asks you to do.

This concept holds true when we consider making a difference in this world. How quickly we forget that the Christian faith was spread and mobilized through Jesus' patient mentoring of 12 men. The idea of changing something that has become so ingrained in our culture almost immediately dials up thoughts such as "impossible" or "that will never happen in my lifetime." It's easy to become paralyzed when looking at such an overwhelming problem. We want to ask ourselves, "Will recycling this soda can really matter? Will replanting a tree make a difference? Will drinking purified water from a cup rather than buying bottled water when it's not absolutely necessary make a significant impact?"

When we are faced with such questions, we have two options: do nothing or get started. In looking at the troubling issues with the way we handle our environment today, we must first admit that we haven't been great environmentalists. I will be the first to raise my hand and say that I have not done my share in the past. But I am taking small steps toward becoming an environmentally conscious person. Instead of drinking bottled water, I drink out of a Nalgene bottle with filtered water when possible. Instead of having to answer the age old question of "paper or plastic?" I take my own bags when I go shopping. Instead of driving my ranch truck to town on a daily basis, I use my smaller, more economical car.

Our journey toward honoring God by caring for his creation begins with the first step, much like one of the world's most well-known environmentalists did when he was tasked with one of the most daunting projects imaginable: build an ark to save the life on planet earth.

NOAH, THE CONSUMMATE ENVIRONMENTALIST

Almost everyone knows the story of Noah, including people who have never studied the Bible in any detail or even call themselves Christians. With the people in the world turning their back on God, God's grace won out over His anger, as He chose to preserve the life of this planet through a man named Noah. Picking a man He could trust, God goes to Noah and asked him to build a boat that would house at least two of every animal.

What an enormous project! When I think about how God sometimes plants seeds of what I first consider to be impossible dreams in my heart, I reflect on what it must have been like for Noah when he dragged that first gopher wood tree to the shop and asked his sons to saw it up into planks because they were going to build a gigantic boat to save the earth from a devastating flood. Was Noah bored with nothing else to do? Was Noah filled with that much faith? Was Noah simply crazy?

Through the way Noah responded and the way others wrote about him later in the Bible, it's easy to see why Noah began—and finished—the seemingly impossible task that God called him to do: Noah had the fear of God in him. Noah had so much respect and reverence for God that if God called him to do something of this magnitude—as crazy as it might sound—he was going to honor God through obedience. Noah said "yes" to God through the act of chopping down a gopher wood tree and beginning to build a boat. (Yes, God began to preserve mankind and the environment by having Noah and his sons chop down trees to build a boat! Ironic, isn't it?)

In Hebrews, Noah was listed among the heroes of the faith, a compilation of those men and women throughout the Bible who did things without the evidence of what they could see. "It was by faith that Noah built an ark to save his family from the flood. He obeyed God, who warned him about something that had never happened before. By his faith he condemned the rest of the world and was made right in God's sight" (Hebrews 11:7). There's something that happens when people of God rise up in faith. They come to an epiphany about something, yet they don't become overwhelmed. They recognize there's not much they can do individually on their own, but they say yes to the Lord and take that first step.

> There's something that happens when people of God rise up in faith. They come to an epiphany about something, yet they don't become overwhelmed.

There is much to learn about God's heart and the importance of stewardship through a closer examination of the life of Noah.

HOW GOD RECYCLES, RESTORES

In Genesis, we uncover a true picture of who Noah is (he

certainly wasn't perfect) and we find a heart that is committed to serving God. We also find the foreshadowing of God's great story of redemption, the one that is still in progress within our own lives as followers of Jesus. And what comes through loud and clear is God's heart: He loves to recycle.

Instead of throwing us away the first time we veer off the path He sets before us, God meets us along the rough terrain we have chosen and points the way home through the midst of our confusion. He is into taking people who are in a poor state of life and purifying and restoring them, making them new. Through such action, we see the heart of God. Stories like Noah's reveal that recycling and redemption is at the very core of the nature of God.

Simply look and see who was on the ark: faithful followers and God's creation. It's what was important to the Lord. We have all pondered the answer to a question like, "If your house was burning down and you could only get one thing out of it, what would it be?" God's creation needed cleansing, but what was He going to save? God wants to restore people so they can have a deeply intimate relationship with Him. And in doing so, He calls us to participate. Likewise, God wants to preserve His creation—and once again, He is calling us to participate.

GOD'S HEART TOWARD CREATION

We know that an omnipotent God could have just thrown His hands in the air and started afresh with a new earth, new people, new galaxies and solar systems. But what happens when God's omnipotence collides with His grace? He powerfully provides a way for redemption.

In the story of Noah, the rainbow is not just his way of leaving an indelible mark on creation; rather, it is his way of showing that his covenants are lasting and unbreakable. However, this covenant wasn't just between God and humanity—it was also between God and His creation.

> I have placed my rainbow in the clouds. It is the sign of my permanent promise to you and to all the earth. When I send clouds over the earth, the rainbow will be seen in the clouds, and I will remember my covenant with you and with everything that lives. Never again will there be a flood that will destroy all life. — Genesis 9:13-15, NIV

God keeps His promise—and as His people, we should endeavor to honor what God thinks is important. In this story, we undoubtedly realize how precious God considers life—all life—and how much God treasures His creation of earth. While the church has increasingly ignored this value of environmental stewardship, it's never too late to take that first step toward saying "yes" to making a difference in this important area of our world.

AGENTS OF CHANGE

If we desire to become agents of change within the church as we address the issue of environmental stewardship, there are a few steps we must take.

1. Revelation and realization. As we read the account of God coming to Noah and tasking him with the project of building the ark in Genesis 6, we see how Noah received a revelation that this was what God was calling him to do. This is revealed through Noah's response to God's litany of things to do in order to save the earth: "So Noah did everything exactly as God had commanded him." (Genesis 6:22).

In a situation where we desire to change something that seems impossible to change, we must also realize the immensity of the problem—and realize that we cannot do it by ourselves. God says, "I want your life and your life together with other people to make a difference." He brings people a revelation—and He brings them a realization of the call that is upon them. This comes to people who are attempting to hear God in the hour in which they live.

When God gives people vision, it's always too big. That's because we need God to accomplish a truly divine vision. In that first phase of revelation, God calls us to something and the reality of the immense problem itself looms large over us. If you look at the world today, it's easy to get paralyzed considering how to change the environmental condition.

> The second part of this revelation is realizing that God is calling you. He wants you to make a difference—to do the impossible.

The second part of this revelation is realizing that God is calling you. He wants you to make a difference—to do the impossible. In my book *Revolutionary Leadership*, I share the story of how I received the vision for what our church in Boise was going be about. I was on a mountainside praying and asking to hear God's voice for my life when I found a yellow balloon in the bushes with a piece of paper inside with the phrase "Let us love one another – 1

John 4:7&8." On the balloon itself was a picture of Noah's Ark. After praying and talking with the Lord about this discovery, I realized that He wanted that to be the driving force behind the vision of our church. Years later as the Lord began to soften my heart toward the area of the environment, He spoke to me again through this balloon, saying, "The value that was in that balloon—the love for people—that's what is in you. But I've also put something on you, which is to care for the earth." That's when I realized that God was calling me to lead our church in this area.

Through this realization, I firmly believe it is a responsibility, not just for me, but for everyone. In all my years of ministry, I have never received the kind of action-oriented response as I did after preaching on this topic and committing to lead our church in this area. When people heard this message, there was something that just resonated in the heart of our church, urging them on to embrace the impossible.

Whenever God gives us a revelation, He always gives us a plan and a strategy. Look at how detailed God was in telling Noah what needed to be done to accomplish this mission in Genesis 6:

> * "Make a boat from resinous wood and seal it with tar, inside and out. Then construct decks and stalls throughout its interior" (vs. 14).
> * "Make it 450 feet long, 75 feet wide, and 45 feet high" (vs. 15).
> * "Construct an opening all the way around the boat, 18 inches below the roof. Then put three decks inside the boat – bottom, middle, and upper – and put a door in the side" (vs. 16).

* "Bring a pair of every kind of animal – a male and a female – into the boat with you to keep them alive during the flood" (vs. 19)
* "Pairs of each kind of bird and each kind of animal, large and small alike, will come to you to be kept alive" (vs. 20)
* "And remember, take enough food for your family and for all the animals" (vs. 21).

God gave Noah a strategic plan to accomplish what he called him to do.

When we feel God calling us to do something, we must be diligent to hold it up to biblical truth. We must ask ourselves, "Is this in alignment with the character and nature of God?" God is into recycling. He is into conservation of people and nature.

We call nature "nature" because it depicts God's nature. All things we see outdoors that are not manmade are a reflection of who He is. When a seed falls to the ground and dies, it is buried but brings forth new life at another time. That is a reflection of God—the analogies are endless. As God calls His church to return to the value of caring for His creation, we see another powerful side of the nature of God—He is a God of restoration, new beginnings, and salvation.

> We call nature "nature" because it is a picture of God's nature. All things we see outdoors that are not manmade are a reflection of who He is.

For generations, God has used imperfect people as agents of change in His world. He called upon Gideon, one of the most timid and fearful men from the weakest tribe, to save

Israel from the marauding Midianites and conquer hundreds of thousands of men with a small army of 300. He used Joshua to convince the Israelites to march around Jericho, the city with invincible walls, for seven days in order to conquer it—and it worked!

Once people receive a vision to do something, the Lord brings the commissioning to them and says, "I want you to make a difference and do something about this." But how much of an impact we make as agents of change depends upon our response.

2. Response and reaction. As we receive vision, the first part is God's part. He casts the vision and directs us on how we should go. The next part of the equation is how we respond. Once the issue is on the table, how will we respond? What will we do about it?

Again, we see Noah's response to God was one of continual obedience:

> Finally, the day came when the Lord said to Noah, "Go into the boat with all your family, for among all the people of the earth, I consider you alone to be righteous. Take along seven pairs of each animal that I have approved for eating and for sacrifice, and take one pair of each of the others. Then select seven pairs of every kind of bird. There must be a male and a female in each pair to ensure that every kind of living creature will survive the flood. One week from today I will begin forty days and forty nights of rain. And I will wipe from the earth all the living things I have created." So Noah did exactly as the Lord had commanded him. — Genesis 7:1-5

Usually, my first response is to freak out! I start to wonder, "How am I going to do this?! Who will help me? This seems overwhelming!" And then, I repent. I'm not simply implying that I repent because my reaction wasn't this immediate one of great faith, but I repent because it puts my heart in a posture of humility before the Lord. When Nehemiah heard about the devastation occurring to the city of Jerusalem, he began to cry out to God and repent for their sins. (See Nehemiah 1:4)

Spiritual and emotional response. Our first response, spiritually and emotionally, must be one of humility, brokenness, and repentance. We must repent for the way in which we have all contributed to the environmental problems—even without our knowing it. And we must enter into this area with humility and brokenness through prayer. Our brokenness gives God the opportunity to make us whole again.

Our first reaction shouldn't be to go out and start some program. Our first response should be to go to him in prayer and say, "Lord, we need you! It's too big for us to do by ourselves!"

Physical response. After we have spent time on our face before the Lord praying about this and the Lord has given us strategy, we must have a "hands and feet" response. In other words, we must begin the work by taking action.

Our first physical response should be one of obedience. In Genesis 6:22 and 7:5, we learn that Noah did everything God commanded him to do. We must first take a step in the right direction, obeying what God has called us to do. In the Bible, we see how God honored small beginnings, even when He sometimes had to prod people to get moving. We simply get started. In Exodus, we find Moses sitting on the cusp of the Red sea and the frantic activity that was going on all around him—and The Living Bible paraphrases what God tells Moses: "Quit praying and get the people moving! Forward, march!" (Exodus 14:15).

Next, we begin to do what we can personally. We want to model this new lifestyle of environmental stewardship for others. So, what do we do?

The first action we can take is developing a habit of recycling or something else that is simple to do. We recycle this bottle or we get a reusable bottle. Even when it seems menial, we must do the right thing. Those actions establish healthy habits from which we can begin to become a sound voice that calls others to similar actions.

What good will it do to drink out of a reusable cup when there are billions of plastic water bottles piling up in landfills? God will bless it. Zechariah says, "Do not despise these small beginnings, for the Lord rejoices to see the work begin, to see the plumb line in Zerubbabel's hand" (Zechariah 4:10). God will bless it when you make a decision to start recycling in your home.

You've got to start somewhere. You've got to do something. You've got to think twice when you throw that thing out of your car window. And please, don't put a bumper sticker on your car promoting care for the environment when it looks like you came out of a toxic dump site when you start up to leave an intersection. Get a new car or repair your old one so that it isn't such a pollutant to the environment. Start somewhere.

As it relates to the church, the next response would be that of calling others to participation. God blesses us when we do things together. I know alone I might not be able to do that much, but when I am of one mind and one heart with people, God can do something great. For the church to simply do the right thing in the area of environmental stewardship will make a difference. We have the opportunity to influence others to do the same.

Within the church, I think we need to do the thing we know how to do and have a reputation for doing—we serve. We serve the communities in which we live with the love and passion of Christ. We need to continue to build upon our reputation of servanthood and let our voice be our example, not necessarily the words that we speak. When we do speak with words, we should have action that backs them.

> Within the church, I think we need to do the thing we know how to do and have a reputation for doing—we serve.

God blesses tenacity, not people who are a flash in the pan. He wants a long, slow burn. As a pastor, I am going to commit myself to being a leader in the area of environmental stewardship over the long haul. We know there will be resistance, even by those in the church who don't understand. But we must commit to leading this cause throughout the corporate body of Christ.

3. Responsibility and accountability. Once God brings a revelation of his vision to us and we respond both spiritually and physically, the next area we enter into is responsibility and accountability. This is where God calls us to the stewardship of His creation.

Stewardship starts with resource and provision. God has

given us a gift. He has given us the earth to dwell on and in to use. When God says, "tend the garden," He doesn't say look at it and don't touch. He says you have to use it and cultivate it, but don't abuse it.

He has given us everything for use and provision. How we use what is given will be important. We are going to be accountable for the environment and for the sanctity of life. That is a very important message. Any time that the church sends the message that we must save people's lives but ignore the environment, it's a conflicting message. These two things have to be brought into balance. And in society today, it's not in balance. People seem to care about the sanctity of life from either the human perspective or the environmental perspective. That is one of the greatest misconceptions the church faces today. The truth is this—God loves life, all life. As Christians, we must be consistently pro-life, which includes caring for the earth.

4. God's covenant. As mentioned earlier in this book, God used the rainbow to establish His covenant not just with people but also with the earth. (Genesis 9:12). When God's covenant is established, there is reconstruction, restoration, reconciliation and resurrection.

When God's covenant is established, a new generation is blessed. When God's covenant is established, change occurs and hope is restored. When God's covenant is established, we experience fulfillment knowing we have invested our lives well.

The Bible tells us that our days our numbered. Our life on earth is short-lived. We are called in a moment and in a breath to make a difference with our lives. And as it relates to the world in which we live, we are called to leave the earth a bet-

ter place than when we found it through a life of good stewardship.

Dr. Jeffrey Greenberg: Raising up Christian Environmental Leaders for the 21st Century

Jeffrey Greenberg spent plenty of time in the outdoors growing up in South Florida. But it wasn't until he was in the middle of writing his doctoral dissertation in geology at the University of North Carolina that he accepted Christ. "While I was working on my dissertation," Greenberg said, "I began to work on my spiritual foundation. And after I became a believer, I realized that my academic side and my spiritual side really came together when it came to caring for creation."

However, as Greenberg entered into the academic world with a fresh perspective, he was tempted into the debate of creation versus evolution. "As a geologist, you are thrown into the controversy," he said. "But I find the whole argument tedious. God gave us something, which you can't argue about—and caring for creation is something that must be done. And as a believer, there was no big revelation moment for me; it just always made a lot of sense to be a good steward of the environment."

Throughout his career, Greenberg has worked in public universities as well as in the public sector, where he served at the Wisconsin Geological and Natural History Survey. But when he took a position at Wheaton College, Greenberg began to see a new way to influence believers to be good environment stewards—train them with the skills necessary to be good stewards professionally.

"Coming to Wheaton with the Christian component already ingrained in them, our students have this wonderful desire to make a difference in the world," Greenberg said. "And sometimes, they're just looking for a direction to merge both their passion for Christ and their passion for people. I've ventured more and more into applications of geology that include human needs and development. And I want to help train students to do this on a professional level and do it with excellence. Academically and spiritually, I have this desire to see something unique that God created rebuilt and re-established—and that has everything to do with people as well."

Greenberg has tackled his fresh calling with a two-pronged approach, seeding the value of environmental stewardship in both traditional classroom settings as well as in non-traditional arenas. For the past few years, Greenberg has taught at University of the Nations sites for Youth With a Mission (YWAM) in Hawaii and South Africa. Through these classes, Greenberg equips missionaries with the tools they need to handle certain environmental concerns in developing nations.

"At these schools, the idea is to help present a world-view and a new perspective on many different issues," Greenberg said. "Specifically, I want to teach them enough about the earth so they understand how it works in order to take care of it properly. If they don't understand the world in which these people live, they will miss an important life connection."

At Wheaton, Greenberg has also overseen some of his students' environmental projects to clean up areas of South African cities along the coast. "What these students were able to do was to clean up these townships in a profound way," Greenberg said. "It helped bring back some pride to one area that is one of the best surfing beaches in the world. While they were beautifying the land, they also helped show the people how they could maintain the area that would be healthy as well. When the world gets sick, people get sick. I want to get them more balanced in their approach to helping people that recognizes both physical and spiritual needs."

In challenging other believers on the topic of environmental stewardship, Greenberg has found that it is an environmental issue that remains the most toxic enemy to public health in the world: water supply. However, he sees these challenges as a way for Christians to enter science and help people in a very tangible way.

"I am terribly biased on this issue," Greenberg said. "But if young Christian adults want to do something to help the world and they want to show the love of Christ at the same time, science and geology in particular are areas with tremendous needs all over the planet—and tremendous opportunities.

"Clean water and water supply is the number one health problem in the world today. And that's the realm of geology. We want people who are looking for something to do who love to help people and share the love of Christ in a very practical way. Today, the biggest topics discussed in the news are energy resources, tsunamis, earthquakes and hurricanes. All of these are geological problems and all of them have opportunities for people to get into these fields and share the gospel through working with people."

Greenberg has seen the level of environmental consciousness rise among Christians in recent years, but he sees room for more progress to be made—even if it means making some waves. "We're so afraid of rocking the boat, but maybe we need to rock the boat," Greenberg said. "There are so many people on the fringe of Christianity, but are so afraid of the Gospel because of the strong conservatism that's grounded more politically than biblically. By embracing environmental stewardship, we have an opportunity to reach people in a way the church hasn't seen in a long time."

Learn more about Greenberg's program at wheaton.edu

CHAPTER SEVEN

Getting to Work

*The heavens declare the glory of God not by speaking in voice audible
to the sensible ears, but by manifesting to us through their own
greatness, the power of the Creator, and when we remark on their
beauty, we give glory to their Maker as the best of all Artificers.*

JOHN DAMASCENE

*The Lord God placed the man in the Garden of Eden
to tend and care for it.*

GENESIS 2:15

Transitioning from good ideas to the implementation of those ideas can sometimes be the greatest challenge we ever face in reshaping our culture. When I was challenged about the state of affairs in my own life regarding the environment as well as the collective view our church held, I wanted to see us move from good ideas regarding environmental stewardship to actually doing it. As much as I wanted to see this value shared by all our church people, I wanted to see it upheld in practical ways that were visible to everyone who walked through our church doors.

Our goal as a church from our inception was to create authentic followers of Jesus—and it always will be our goal. Sometimes, however, shifts in our approach to ministry must be made. After much strategizing, planning, recruiting, implementation and accountability, we have managed to begin shifting the culture of our church in the way our people collectively view the environment. Instead of the environment being at odds with their faith, they realize how its care fits comfortably into a life of total stewardship. But this process hasn't been easy.

SHIFTING ESTABLISHED PERCEPTIONS

As God began to speak to me about the topic of environmental stewardship, I began to change my own thinking. During this process, I realized that a transformation needed to occur in our church as well. So, I began the strategic process.

Brainstorming. When we recognize something as God's leading in your life, we can't drag our feet about it. We must begin devising a plan to arrive at the destination God is calling us to.

Living in Idaho, there are many people within our church who are involved in environmental conservation efforts, some through government agencies and other through non-profit organizations. So, I devised a think-tank of sorts, gathering people together and asking them how we could raise this value in our church and give practical ways for people to get involved. In a matter of weeks, I think I uncovered all our closet environmentalists and asked them to get involved with this planning and strategy. There are people who are consummate lovers of creation in every church. Getting these people on the ground floor of developing an environmental ministry in your church is vital to your success. If you're one of these people, begin looking for like-minded church members who desire to see this value elevated and start planning.

Start somewhere. Like most cultures, church cultures do not change overnight. Gradually introducing ideas of ways to care for the environment into your church and community will begin to take the people in the congregation toward understanding and adopting the value of environmental stewardship.

As our church staff began to talk about this issue, we realized that we had a vast number of opportunities to make small changes. One of the first things we did was simple enough— we added recycling bins for aluminum cans in our building. Then we added recycling bins for other products such as plastic bottles. From our office standpoint, we realized a simple way to make a statement about our shifting values was to print our bulletin on post-consumer recycled paper. It was something small that we could do that spoke volumes about the direction we were heading as a church.

Build momentum as the ministry grows. At first, there may be some push back by people in the church who don't understand this value or why a church would be involved with something so seemingly out of character with its "traditional" values. However, as people begin to warm to the idea that caring for the earth is a basic biblical value, the environmental ministry in your church will begin to grow.

As this value began to become more and more vivid in the church, we shifted gears, adding more layers of depth to environmental stewardship. Instead of simply recycling aluminum cans, we began to implement other practical applications of conservation and stewardship. Through ideas our think tank developed, we rolled out opportunities to hit the backwoods trails and pull noxious weeds in the wilderness areas. We offered individuals and families the chance to go camping and clean up campgrounds or hiking trails in the foothills. People could also participate by hiking trails with a GPS navigational device to help the U.S. Forest Service in checking the accuracy of their topographical maps.

Educate people. As in any cultural shift of this magnitude (we're talking about undoing misconceptions some people have held about the environment for their entire lives), education plays a vital role. If stewardship is a value that is upheld from the pulpit in your church, encourage those teaching on the subject to share the importance of environmental stewardship just like they would stewardship of our finances. It is also important to provide people with a deeper understanding of not only why they should care for the earth but how.

Our church's leadership team developed a four-week course that outlines why Christians should care for the earth as well as how they can do it. (This resource will be available at www.savinggodsgreenearth.com) Many people do not know that there are different types of recyclable plastics, categorized through a numeric system. If people don't know that No. 5 plastics don't mix with No. 2 plastics at the recycling bin (or know where to look on the plastic goods to find that information), they can cause more work or contaminate other recycled goods. People also may not know the difference between a product that is labeled "made with recycled paper" and one labeled "made with post-consumer recycled paper." There are practical things people should know about recycling that will help them be well-informed as well as be knowledgeable when passing this information along to others.

Share this value with others. Once you begin to see what type of impact caring for creation will have not only in your own life but also on the life of your church, don't shy away from sharing this with others in communities of faith around your area. Just like when you partner together with others in any Spirit-led venture, God seems to multiply your efforts in exponential ways.

We reach more people and accomplish more work when we partner with other people instead of trying to blaze our own trail. Invite friends and families as well as other churches to participate in environmental clean-ups or other activities that call people to take individual action with a corporate body. For example, you may choose to join others in your community on Earth Day, caring for the environment side by side those who think that Christians don't care about the earth. Look for opportunities in your community to reach out through means of environmental stewardship.

Our church found current initiatives taking place in the community and joined in. We realized that we didn't need to make this value "Christian" by developing it ourselves—environmental stewardship is already a Christian value. So, why not join what is already happening in your community? When we did this, we became the leading supplier of volunteers to a number of different initiatives. Suddenly, we developed a reputation for being a church that cared about its community and were asked to participate in other projects as well, some of which weren't directly related to the environment.

Continue to cast the vision. After a full year of teaching on this value, promoting this value, and giving people in our church the opportunity participate on many different levels in raising this value in their own lives and in their community, we recast the vision. Through a documentary our staff developed, we were able to tell the story all over again about what it means to care for creation, what it looks like, and how people can help. For people who were new to our church, they were able to see with greater detail how important this value was for us and see new opportunities for them to implement it in their own lives.

Celebrate. God loves to celebrate. It is part of His DNA that He has written into the heart of every man, woman, and child. People love to celebrate. We should celebrate God's creation on a regular basis, upholding the beauty that is uniquely marked with His fingerprints. Holding a meeting one Sunday outside in a park or hosting a picnic outdoors for the sheer purpose of getting people outside to enjoy God's beautiful creation is a great way to do this.

As you begin to take up the value of environmental stewardship in your own life, you will undoubtedly want to share it with others. And while these are just a few suggestions in helping you begin to walk down this path with your church, the ways to help care for God's creation are seemingly limitless. In the "Garden Shed" section of the book, you will find some creative ideas that you may be able to implement in your church as well. There are also more ideas listed at the book's website: www.savinggodsgreenearth.com.

Our church has adopted a saying that we use as the mantra for our environmental ministry: *God's Creation. Our Responsibility.* My hope is that you see the truth in this statement as well, realizing just how amazing God's creation truly is and just how awesome the responsibility we have as His people to take care of it.

CHAPTER EIGHT

The Garden Shed: Practical Ideas

Listen to the sermon preached to you by the flowers, the trees, the shrubs, the sky, and the whole world. Notice how they preach to you a sermon full of love, of praise of God, and how they invite you to glorify the sublimity of that sovereign Artist who has given them being.

PAUL OF THE CROSS

He existed before everything else began, and he holds all creation together.

COLOSSIANS 1:17

T he Garden Shed serves as a small resource center for you in starting an environmental ministry at your church or simply implementing ways to care for creation in your own personal life. This guide is divided into two sections: individual participation and group activities. Many of the individual participation ideas are ones that can be established church-wide but still call for people to get involved on a personal basis.

These are only a select few ideas. You may find more at www.savinggodsgreenearth.com or log on and share your own.

INDIVIDUAL RESPONSE

Begin Recycling. One simple thing everyone can do is begin recycling all possible products you buy if you don't already. And you can recycle more than just aluminum cans and newspapers. Plastic bags, white paper, colored paper, tin cans, glass bottles, cardboard boxes and magazines are just a handful of items that people don't necessarily think about recycling that can be recycled just as easily as aluminum cans and newspapers. Your community may provide curbside recycling on some of the items listed above but not all of them—and some places may require you to sort the items before dropping them off at the curb.

If you're not sure what you can recycle in your community, www.earth911.org is a great resource website where you can find out for your area what's available to be recycled and what isn't.

Stop unsolicited mailing. Eco-cycle claims that in the U.S. each year junk mail requires 80 million trees and uses 28 billion gallons of water to produce it—and it costs approximately $450 million to take all of these mailings to a recycling center. There are also estimates that we spend an average of eight months of our lives dealing with junk mail—who wouldn't want to stop this?

At www.eco-cycle.org, you will find in-depth information in how to reduce the amount of "junk mail" delivered to your home each week. One of the ways suggested to stop those relentless credit card offers is to visit the website www.optout-prescreen.com to get your name removed from the mailing list of creditors and insurers. You can also call visit the Direct Marketing Association's website at www.dmaconsumers.org to be removed from the "mother list."

Carpool. Americans love their freedom more than any other nation on the planet as evidenced by the highest automobile per capita ratio. One way to conserve fuel and prevent needless emissions is by carpooling. Some employers and many states offer financial incentives for people to carpool, particularly in metro areas. Check with your state department of transportation office to see if your state offers such incentives.

Reusable resources. Make the switch from consumption of resources to reusable resources. For example, instead of carting home 8-10 plastic bags each time you go to the grocery store, bring your own cloth bags, which will hold up much better than the plastic ones any way. (However, many places will allow you to recycle your plastic grocery bags—and some will even reward you for it.) Instead of drinking water out of bottles you will soon throw away, begin using a durable hard plastic bottle that you fill at home with filtered water when it is convenient. Instead of taking your lunch to work in plastic bags, try using some type of reusable plastic containers.

CORPORATE RESPONSE

Recycle as a church. Earlier in the book, I mentioned that our staff begin developing ways to move our people into action in the area of environmental stewardship. One of the ways we did this was through a recycling program called "Tithe Your Trash." This program has been a huge success with our people since our area currently has no curbside recycling program for many of the items people can recycle. We searched for the major recycling center in our area that would take a multitude of recycled projects and began taking our church recycled goods there each week. We set up a team to receive and sort the trash, something that must be done when it is dropped off at the recycling center. This opportunity is made available to people before and after each service—and it happens right near the front door. It immediately communicates our heart as a church to be leaders in the area of caring for creation to those who are coming to our church for the first time.

While many people in your church may recycle already or your area has a curbside recycling program, another way to recycle is to place aluminum can recycling bins in your church lobby near each trash receptacle. You may also want to consider placing paper recycling bins by the doors so people can recycle their bulletins (printed on recycled paper, right?) each Sunday on the way out the church doors.

Recycle cell phones; fund your ministries. Cell phones and other electronic devices contain many toxic substances, such as beryllium, cadmium, copper, lead, nickel, and zinc, which tend to stay in the soil for a longer period of time before breaking down. The good news is that much of these substances can be recycled—and they can be done in such a way that you can raise money for your organization. There are a number of companies such as Charitablerecycling.org, Wirelessrecycling.com, and Eco-cell.org which will exchange cell phones for cash to your non-profit organization.

As I shared in Chapter 4, after Hurricane Katrina hit, our church seized the opportunity to invite our community to participate in our outreach efforts in the Gulf Coast region through donating cell phones to fund our actions there. Cleaning up after Katrina in and of itself was a major environmental undertaking, but utilizing an environmental concern to serve people through another environmental concern—and receiving funding to do it—enabled our church to send teams to the area for 14 straight weeks with minimum financial obligation from our church.

The way we went about this project was by asking our home groups to hang bags (made of recycled paper, of course) on the doors of people in the neighborhoods and apartment complexes explaining how they could contribute to helping the environment and helping the victims of Hurricane Katrina. A note on the bag let the people know when our church members would return to pick them up. It was encouraging to see the way that many people who weren't believers responded to our outreach, gladly contributing their cell phones—and then engaged many of our church members in conversations about why Christians would care about the environment. We even had businesses and government organizations donating their phones to the cause, bringing boxes of old cell phones to our church. It truly was an amazing response.

Empower your church with recyclable items. As I mentioned earlier in the book, when our church was looking for creative ways to care for the environment and share our faith, our team came up with the idea of developing reusable "green bags" for grocery shopping. Using bags made of reusable material, we put our environmental ministry logo on the side and sold them in bundles of six at a low cost to encourage people to participate. Soon people in our congregation began to report stories of being approached by strangers in the store, first inquiring about the bags and then inquiring about why Christians would care for the environment. Since our church holds high the value of discipleship, it was easy for the church to share their faith in the midst of these conversations.

Get outdoors. One thing I've learned is that people won't appreciate something as much until they have experienced it. And experiencing the outdoors is something people need to do in order to develop a passion to properly care for it. To begin to instill this value in our church, I asked people to enlarge personal pictures of them enjoying the outdoors and bring them to church for display in our lobby for an art exhibit. If people didn't have any pictures, I encouraged them to get out there so they could take some. The point of the exercise was to remind people of how much they enjoy God's beautiful creation—and get them back outside more often. Certain ministries in your church can promote corporate camping trips, allowing your church to accomplish connecting people to God through nature and connecting to one another.

Find environmental projects and get involved. In our desire to get involved as a church through different opportunities available to the public, we asked the U.S. Forest Service how we could help. Though government funded, the U.S. Forest Service has many more projects than they have people to accomplish them, so they welcomed our open invitation to serve on some projects during the summer. Teams from our church went into the Idaho wilderness area and pulled noxious weeds. Other teams restored campgrounds or performed maintenance on 25 miles of trails. We also had other smaller teams volunteer to hike trails with GPS tracking devices to verify the authenticity of certain topographical maps.

Within the city of Boise, our church had teams involved in a project called "Re-Leaf Boise," where large trees were replanted in strategic areas. In a parks and recreation department project, our youth served by putting out mulch and repainting a park. And then there were teams who cleaned up along the river and repaired trails in the foothills. There was something available for every age and interest—and the response we received from the church was incredible.

Adopt-a-highway. Most state transportation departments will allow an organization or a family to adopt a portion of a state highway for clean up purposes. This is an excellent opportunity for you to continue to see the value of caring for creation within your church by calling people to corporate participation. It may not seem like much, but people will soon begin to take pride in their strip of the road—and the value will become more real to them on a personal level as well.

Get an energy audit. Organizations such as Interfaith Power & Light (which has a growing number of branches in various states) will perform an energy audit at your church, giving you suggestions and ideas on how to reduce the amount of needless energy consumption that occurs in your facility. And the money your church saves can go toward advancing the Kingdom.

www.savinggodsgreenearth.com Visit the book's website to sign up for more ideas as well as a monthly newsletter about other opportunities for environmental stewardship on both individual and corporate levels.

A NEW APPROACH TO OUTREACH

As John Wimber used to say, "The meat is in the street," meaning that real growth in our lives as Christian occurs when we are serving others. In regards to environmental stewardship, the "meat" is also in the hills, rivers, valleys, and mountains. There's something unique about using environmental community service to show others the beauty of the Creator. Many people are often enamored with the beauty of the world around them, yet they haven't yet met the Creator. While our church continues to use acts of love and kindness as a way to share God's love with people, environmental ministry outreach not only puts believers in the community but it puts them working hand in hand with those who have not yet received Christ. In outreach, making the connection and building relationships is 90 percent of the work—and usually the hardest. Eventually, when other people begin to see the light of Jesus alive in us, the opportunities to share our faith will come ... and they come at their request.

Since we have embarked on becoming a church that is environmentally conscious through adhering to environmental stewardship, our staff has received numerous reports of how this has affected the community and drawn many unbelievers to our church. I sincerely believe God's hand is upon the idea of environmental stewardship for many reasons, including His desire for us to care for his creation in a responsible way and His desire to see people come to know Him.

In our current culturally and politically divided landscape, it is difficult to fight through the portrait the media paints of Christians because of either their own agendas or the vocal minority that doesn't always represent what it means to follow Jesus in the best light. What breaks down stereotypes and softens hearts are personal relationships where people who have been led to believe all Christians believe and act a certain way suddenly realize that those who truly follow Jesus are distinctly different. It is my prayer that on both on individual basis and on a corporate level, you will begin to see transformation occur in your heart through the power of the Holy Spirit working in and through you as you share the love of Christ through the value of caring for God's creation.

Let's Tend the Garden

The little birds singing are signing of God; the beasts cry unto Him; the elements are in awe of Him; the mountains echo His name; the waves and streams cast their glances at Him; the herbs and flowers praise Him. Nor do we need to labor or seek Him far off, since each one of us finds (God) within himself, inasmuch as we are all upheld and preserved by His power dwelling in us.

JOHN CALVIN

In my previous book, *Revolutionary Leadership*, I shared the concept of synergistic leadership. It was my hope to illustrate how the symbiotic interaction of the three components of vision, culture and structure—when properly execute—would stimulate a whirlwind of charismatic activity and build momentum in church ministry. In the 25 years that I have participated in full-time Christian leadership, I have never experienced this phenomenon more than in the development of our environmental ministry, Let's Tend the Garden (LTTG). At the conclusion of our first year of work on LTTG, I approached Brandon, a young man on our church staff who oversees all of our technical production. Brandon is the guy responsible for creative video each week to promote various ministries on Sunday mornings and all other events. I asked him to gather any available video clips and pictures from our various environmental projects during the year and organize the material into a thirty minute documentary presentation for the church. It was my intention at the time to have something visual to share in order to recast the vision and thus re-stimulate our church culture so that we could plan for another year of fruitful ministry.

Brandon diligently worked on the assignment and when completed, he called me in to see his first draft of the documentary. As I observed what he had done tears welled up in my eyes. Not only had Brandon captured and documented one of the best examples of synergy I have personally experienced, but he reminded me of how much God had done to establish this new work. Brandon began the film with excerpts of that first Sunday when I had so nervously shared my heart with our church concerning the commission for Christian environmental stewardship. He went on to interview various participants who had captured this vision and helped establish it as a part of our church culture. He showed the hundreds of people who participated in the various outreaches and projects throughout the community, and in the forests and wilderness of Idaho. It overwhelmed me to realize how much had been accomplished in just one short year. Not only had we affected our own church culture, but we had attracted the attention of people far beyond our walls. Articles have been written on our environmental work in national magazines and newspapers; there have also been multiple interviews on both local and nation radio and television. Because of our website (www.letstendthegarden.org) people across the country are e-mailing and calling our office for resource and for the purpose of building new partnerships.

Through all the swirl of activity this ministry has generated, I realize that Christian environmental stewardship was a sleeping giant just waiting to be awakened. I have also discovered that there are numbers of Christian environmental parachurch organizations but few that are operating directly within local churches. It has also become evident that all that was needed were a few successful models for others to observe and follow. As one pastor friend of mine put it, "We were waiting to see if someone else could survive being 'green' without being labeled a wacko before we stepped in."

We have not only survived but we have discovered a veritable vein of untapped gold. The morning our people gave me a standing ovation for my first "green" message made me realize that not only was the church ecstatic, but God was pleased as well. The Lord has been looking for a group of courageous leaders to step out of a falsely constructed conservative box and re-embrace His commission to care for His creation. When we did our part, He did His. He breathed on the work of our hands and did the work of His. As a result the ministry accelerated and built momentum beyond my wildest dreams.

Now, after a year of ministry, environmental stewardship has become a normal part of our church culture. No one feels weird or even radical; we just feel we are being obedient. "Let's Tend the Garden" has attracted people we would have never had the privilege of introducing to Christ; and it has given us a new kind of credibility in our state. We have provided a means for Christian people who previously had a heart for the environment to come out from behind the 'trees or rocks' where they have been hiding, giving them the opportunity to express their passion in legitimate church ministry.

Our dream is to see churches across the country and around the world join us in this noble effort. We know there are many churches that have already been doing this work, but we want to connect like-minded and like hearted partners. If enough churches join together I believe environmental stewardship will be re-established as a normal value of Christianity. If this happens we would surely begin to see changes in our world. Polluted water would be cleaned up, helping 80 percent of the world's diuretic disease to decline; soil would be rejuvenated and starvation in the developing countries would begin to turn around. Church missions programs would develop discipleship programs made up of thousands of young people who could form agencies much like the Peace Corp but no longer secular. These new agencies would go into the world not only with proclamation of the Gospel, but with physical demonstration of care, compassion and mercy. Young people today are crying out to see the church embrace programs of social justice that provide something tangible to participate in.

Together, the body of Christ could do what no other single independent organization could possibly hope to accomplish. With God's blessing and the power of His Holy Spirit, the Church could join hands in the 21st Century and be the very first truly effective international workforce of environmental stewardship around this globe.

The hour is late, the need is urgent; God is stirring His people to break down dividing walls so that we might work together in unity to "tend His garden."

OTHER AMPELON PUBLISHING TITLES

God's Relentless Pursuit: Discovering His Heart for Humanity
by Phil Strout
retail price: $10.95

Have you ever considered that instead of us chasing God, He is actually the One chasing us? In his book, author Phil Strout explores God's mission on earth and how His people join in His mission: to draw people into relationship with Him. Many common ideas and notions regarding our role in pursuing God are challenged as we discover the truth about what God is doing in and around us, both across the street and across the oceans.

Sample chapters and book are available for purchase at: www.ampelonpublishing.com

Passionate Pursuit: Discovering the Heart of Christ
by Jason Chatraw
retail price: $9.95

Do you want to experience a greater intimacy in the time you spend with God? If so, the devotional *Passionate Pursuit* helps set you on the right path. We must know that our relationship with God is a journey, not a quick trip. And being equipped for the journey will make it more fun and exciting.

Sample chapters and book are available for purchase at: www.ampelonpublishing.com

OTHER AMPELON PUBLISHING TITLES

Revolutionary Leadership
by Tri Robinson
retail price: $12.95

Is your church growing? More importantly, is your church creating authentic followers of Jesus? In *Revolutionary Leadership*, author and pastor Tri Robinson shares his journey of planting a church that is serious about discipleship. Out of his desire to pastor a church that was intentional and successful at developing passionate followers of Jesus, Robinson discovered the concept of synergy and how its components can help revolutionize leadership within a church.

Sample chapters and book are available for purchase at: www.ampelonpublishing.com

SEE A SAMPLE CHAPTER FOR REVOLUTIONARY LEADERSHIP ON THE FOLLOWING PAGES.

This is a sample chapter from Tri Robinson's book, Revolutionary Leadership.

Revolutionary Leadership

CHAPTER ONE

]magine the possibilities of what can happen when God begins to transform a community. It is infinite what God can do when His people are both individually and corporately devoted to   following Him. For me, the endless possibilities started with a deflated helium balloon.

In the early spring of 1987, Michael Anderson was 12 years old. He stood on the front lawn of his church in Ontario, Oregon, holding a yellow, helium-filled balloon prepared earlier that morning in his Sunday School class. Inside the balloon, he had inserted a scrap of notebook paper with the handwritten words, "Let us love one another – 1 John 4:7 & 8." He released his balloon along with the rest of the class. It slowly rose into the cold morning air, drifting eastward with the prevailing wind toward the Idaho border.

A little over a year later in the summer of 1988, the last thing on my mind was planting a church in Idaho. My wife, Nancy, and I were happily situated in a growing Vineyard church in Southern California. We felt secure and fulfilled in our ministry as associate pastors at the Desert Vineyard Christian Fellowship in Lancaster, California.

Nancy and I fell in love 20 years earlier when we met as students at the College of Idaho (now Albertson College) in Caldwell, Idaho. We married in 1970 and remained in Caldwell as newlyweds for two more years before moving to the mountains of California to raise our children on my family's ranch. I went to work as a schoolteacher for several years before joining the church staff in Lancaster.

In 1988, we received a phone call from an old Idaho friend. Pat Armstrong, who had remained close with Nancy and me since our college days, made his living building backcountry trails with a team of mules. We had often spent several of our summer breaks working for Pat while I was still teaching school.

At the time I received Pat's phone call, we hadn't worked for him in several years due to our responsibilities at the church. However, he called to ask for help on a project to reconstruct a damaged airstrip on the Middle Fork of the Salmon River. With a couple of weeks of vacation, we jumped at the opportunity and headed 800 miles north to Idaho. Our kids, Kate and Brook, had heard many stories about our early days in Idaho but had never visited the state themselves. We were all content with our lifestyle on the family ranch. None of us had even considered leaving our comfortable California lifestyle – that is, until we passed through Boise on our way to meet Pat.

Vision never announces its coming, but when it comes, you know it. And before I knew it, vision was on my front porch, knocking loudly on the door.

I can't explain what happened that day, but I believe it was supernatural – our whole family fell in love with the city. God was definitely doing something in all of our hearts, but I was the last to admit it. Privately, Nancy asked me if I would ever consider giving up our life in California to plant a Vineyard church in Boise. Suddenly, fear began to stir in me because I had witnessed so many church plant failures. Without much thought, I defiantly answered, "No!" And I informed her that I didn't want to talk about it again.

Two days later, we flew into Pat's camp on Mahoney Creek. Everyone was enjoying the time in the wilderness, except me. I was miserable. For many years, I had waited to get back to the mountains of Idaho, but I was not enjoying it. The thought of leaving the security of my established life really bothered me. Leaving the ranch, risking everything, transplanting our family to an unknown place with no friends – it all seemed totally crazy and impractical.

Noticing my struggle, Nancy suggested that I take a long walk and get alone with God. Because of my attitude, I perceived her as really saying, "Why don't you take a hike?" Climbing a tall mountain adjacent to Mahoney Creek, I only stopped to catch my breath and pray. At one point, I remember crying out to God for an answer.

"Lord," I said, "I desperately need a word from you." But every time I stopped hiking, I never heard His voice. Then I figured God would speak to me once I made it to the summit, just as He spoke to Moses on Mt. Sinai. But His voice was absolutely quiet. Finally, I decided to stop guessing how God would speak to me and just enjoy the time I had in the backcountry with my family and friends.

As I began walking down an aspen-covered ridge, something caught my eye on the opposite side of the ravine. The bright yellow object looked out of place for the colors on the mountain terrain. Intrigued by this object, I ventured closer to see what it was.

I descended the ravine and scrambled up the opposite side. After climbing under a thorny berry bush, I emerged carrying Michael Anderson's deflated yellow balloon with an illustration of Noah's ark printed on the side. I sensed this particular balloon had been sent to me from the Lord and that it contained a message in it from Him. I felt the balloon and there was a small note inside. At first, I was almost afraid to remove it. I climbed back up the side of the ravine to a bright sunny spot and sat down. I ripped a small hole on the side of the balloon to remove the paper.

Here I was, sitting on a mountainside in the very center of the largest wilderness area in the continental United States. I had prayed all day for a word from God. As you can guess, the note read, "Let us love one another – 1 John 4:7 & 8." Oddly enough, at the time I remember telling the Lord that

I needed a real word, a more specific answer to my question.

It was then that the Lord spoke to me through the Holy Spirit more clearly than I had ever heard Him before. He said, "Tri, I don't care where you do it. All I want you to do is build a church that loves people." Then He asked me, "Do you want to do it in Boise, Idaho?" It was at that moment that I discovered what He had already put in my heart. Without hesitating, I replied, "Yes, Lord, I do."

Later that morning, I wandered back into our camp at Mahoney Creek and found Nancy by the fire. She asked me if I had heard anything from the Lord. I pulled the balloon and small strip of notebook paper from my pocket, telling her that God had written me a note.

What God was giving me was a vision I couldn't accomplish on my own or even with just my family. I needed several others to journey with me and make this vision from God a reality in the city of Boise. It was almost one year to the day from finding the balloon that we found ourselves back in Boise with 13 other families from the Lancaster church. They, too, felt God's call to go plant a church in Boise that would love people. This team of people would have not been able to fulfill this vision had they gone out alone. But together, we were a collection of believers who trusted that God was going to help us accomplish the purpose He had set before us.

Today, Michael Anderson's balloon is framed on my office wall. I often look at that note and remember God's faithfulness and His very clear commission for us to build a church where people love one another.

On a recent autumn day I had a moment of nostalgia that filled my heart with gratitude. Like many pastors, I often get so focused on the daily responsibilities of running a church that I forget to reflect on the miracles that God has done.

It was a Wednesday and I had just been to the Barnabas Center, our benevolence and outreach facility on our campus. I considered everything I had just observed, ministry and activity in every corner of the facility. I was aware that even though it was mid-morning on a weekday, the food pantry had many volunteers serving and distributing food to numerous needy families. In an adjoining area medical volunteers were working in our free clinic that provided medical assistance to people who couldn't afford it. In the hallway interpreters were interacting with Spanish-speaking clients. There was a team using a fork lift, unloading and moving pallets of food that not only supplied our warehouse but over 25 other food pantries in the community as well. In an adjacent classroom, there were 26 young people being instructed and trained to be missionaries. They would soon be deployed as medics and midwives in poverty-stricken communities. Behind the Barnabas Center, other people were harvesting vegetables in a large garden that supplied the food pantry with fresh produce for the poor.

As I walked back to my office from the Barnabas Center, I paused for a moment on a grass embankment that borders our athletic fields. I took advantage of this vantage point for a quick look around. From my viewpoint, I observed how our elementary school teachers lovingly interacted with their students as they participated in an outside activity. I then turned to look at our main facility – a system of buildings that houses numerous groups every week as well as multiple services on Sundays.

Centered between the children's wing and the administration/adult education wing is a large sanctuary, a youth chapel and a big lobby we lovingly refer to as "Heritage Hall." Heritage Hall is what you might call the living room of the church. It was designed with the idea that church would be an all-week event. The main purpose of the hall is a warm, welcoming place for anyone who wants to hang out. It has a beautiful fireplace, flanked by leather couches and chairs, a coffee bar, a bookstore, and bistro tables complete with plug-ins for computers and Internet access. Often, someone is softly playing the baby grand piano sitting in the corner.

Standing there, viewing this place called Vineyard Boise, it struck me what God can do with a group of people committed to a life of discipleship. I became overwhelmed as I thought about all those who flow through this place on a weekly basis, people who faithfully work in so many areas to bring healing to the broken and hurting, the hundreds of people it takes to lead discipleship groups, children's ministries, youth programs and Bible studies. I thought of those who usher and greet as well as those who serve in the coffee bar week after week. It is truly a busy place.

As I pondered all of this, it struck me how much had happened since that day, many years ago, when I stood on a mountainside in the Idaho wilderness clutching a small yellow balloon. Finding this balloon inspired a clear vision to go build a church that would love people in the name of Jesus. I believe the greatest miracle isn't the size of Vineyard Boise or even the amount of ministry that pours out of it. Instead, it is the miraculous way that God has gathered so many to one place who have captured His heart and desire to be used by Him. Somehow, Vineyard Boise had become a 22-acre campus that facilitates literally hundreds of volunteers who were dedicated to the vision of building a church that would "love people." Only God could have done such a thing.

As I stood there, I realized what an incredible testimony this church is to the power of a God-given vision, a vision that had miraculously become reality in our life at Vineyard Boise.

Throughout this book, we're going to hear some of the real-life stories of people serving in our church who have experienced this radical transformation first-hand. But churches that change lives don't just happen overnight. You can't plant a church and hope to see it grow to a thousand members in a year. Not only is that extremely unlikely, it's also dangerous. Without the proper structure in place, a church can become little more than a popular place to visit on Sundays.

Every church leader wants to see his church or ministry grow, not because they desire to have a big ministry, but because they want to impact more lives for the Kingdom of God. Our discussion throughout this book about vision, culture, and structure will help equip you to develop the momentum you need to fulfill the vision God has placed on your heart. I trust these words will not be just another book full of ideas but practical advice that will change the way you lead in ministry.

To order this book, visit ampelonpublishing.com or buy it at fine Christian bookstores everywhere.